WRITING SKILLS CURRICULUM LIBRARY

Ready-to-Use
PREWRITING & ORGANIZATIONAL Activities

UNIT 4

JACK UMSTATTER

Illustrations by Maureen Umstatter

THE CENTER FOR APPLIED RESEARCH IN EDUCATION
West Nyack, New York 10994

D1247428

Library of Congress Cataloging-in-Publication Data

Umstatter, Jack.
    Writing skills curriculum library / Umstatter, Jack.
       p.   cm.
    Contents: Unit 1. Ready-to-use word activities
    ISBN 0-87628-482-9
    1. English language—Composition and exercises—Study and teaching
(Secondary)—United States.   2 Education, Secondary—Activity
programs—United States.   I. Title.
LB1631.U49 1999
808'.042'0712—dc21
                                       99-21556
                                         CIP

© 1999 by The Center for Applied Research in Education

Printed in the United States of America

10 9 8 7 6 5 4 3 2 1

ISBN 0-87628-485-3

**The Center for Applied Research
in Education**
West Nyack, NY 10994

http://www.phdirect.com

DEDICATED

To John and Mary Umstatter, my father and mother,
for their love, hard work and sense of humor

ACKNOWLEDGMENTS

Thanks to my daughter Maureen for her artistic creativity and to my wife Chris for her many hours of work on this project. I couldn't have done it without you.

Thanks to Connie Kallback and Win Huppuch for their support and encouragement with this series.

Appreciation and thanks to Diane Turso for her meticulous development and copyediting and to Mariann Hutlak, production editor, for her tireless attention throughout the project.

A special thanks to my students, past and present, who inspire these ideas and activities.

Thanks to Terry from WISCO COMPUTING of Wisconsin Rapids, Wisconsin 54495 for his programs.

Definitions for certain words are taken from *Webster's New World Dictionary, Third College Edition* (New York: Simon & Schuster, Inc., 1988).

ABOUT THE AUTHOR

Jack Umstatter has taught English on both the junior high and senior high school levels since 1972, and education and literature at Dowling College (Oakdale, New York) for the past nine years. He currently teaches English in the Cold Spring Harbor School District in New York.

Mr. Umstatter graduated from Manhattan College with a B.A. in English and completed his M.A. in English at S.U.N.Y.—Stony Brook. He earned his Educational Administration degree at Long Island University.

Mr. Umstatter has been selected Teacher of the Year several times and was elected to *Who's Who Among America's Teachers*. Most recently, he appeared in *Contemporary Authors*. Mr. Umstatter has taught all levels of secondary English classes including the Honors and Advanced Placement classes. As coach of the high school's Academic team, the Brainstormers, he led the team in capturing the Long Island and New York State championships when competing in the American Scholastic Competition Network National Tournament of Champions in Lake Forest, Illinois.

Mr. Umstatter's other publications include *Hooked on Literature!* (1994), *201 Ready-to-Use Word Games for the English Classroom* (1994), *Brain Games!* (1996), and *Hooked on English!* (1997), all published by The Center for Applied Research in Education.

ABOUT THE WRITING SKILLS CURRICULUM LIBRARY

According to William Faulkner, a writer needs three things—experience, observation, and imagination. As teachers, we know that our students certainly have these essentials. Adolescents love to express themselves in different ways. Writing is undoubtedly one of these modes of expression. We stand before potential novelists, poets, playwrights, columnists, essayists, and satirists (no comment!). How to tap these possibilities is our task.

The six-unit *Writing Skills Curriculum Library* was created to help your students learn the elements of effective writing and enjoy the experience at the same time. This series of progressive, reproducible activities will instruct your students in the various elements of the writing process as it fosters an appreciation for the writing craft. These stimulating and creative activities also serve as skill-reinforcement tools. Additionally, since the lesson preparation has already been done, you will be able to concentrate on guiding your students instead of having to create, develop, and sequence writing exercises.

- Unit 1, *Ready-to-Use Word Activities*, concentrates on the importance of word selection and exactness in the writing process. William Somerset Maugham said, "Words have weight, sound, and appearance; it is only by considering these that you can write a sentence that is good to look at and good to listen to." Activities featuring connotations, denotations, prefixes, roots, suffixes, synonyms, antonyms, and expressions will assist your students in becoming more conscientious and selective "verbivores," as Richard Lederer would call them. Diction, syntax, and specificity are also emphasized here.

- The renowned essayist, philosopher, and poet, Ralph Waldo Emerson, commented on the necessity of writing effective sentences. He said, "For a few golden sentences we will turn over and actually read a volume of four or five hundred pages." Knowing the essentials of the cogent sentence is the focus of Unit 2, *Ready-to-Use Sentence Activities*. Here a thorough examination of subjects, predicates, complements, types of sentences, phrases, clauses, punctuation, capitalization, and agreement situations can be found. Problems including faulty subordination, wordiness, split infinitives, dangling modifiers, faulty transition, and ambiguity are also addressed within these activities.

- "Every man speaks and writes with the intent to be understood." Samuel Johnson obviously recognized the essence of an effective paragraph. Unit 3, *Ready-to-Use Paragraph Writing Activities*, leads the students through the steps of writing clear, convincing paragraphs. Starting with brainstorming techniques, these activities also emphasize the importance of developing effective thesis statements and topic sentences, selecting an appropriate paragraph form, organizing the paragraph, introducing the paragraph, utilizing relevant supporting ideas, and concluding the paragraph. Activities focusing on methods of developing a topic—description, exemplification, process, cause and effect, comparison-contrast, analogy, persuasion, and definition—are included.

- "General and abstract ideas are the source of the greatest errors of mankind." Jean-Jacques Rousseau's words befit Unit 4, *Ready-to-Use Prewriting & Organization Activities*, for here the emphasis is on gathering and using information intelligently. Activities include sources of information, categorization, topics and sub-topics, summaries, outlines, details, thesis statements, term paper ideas, and formats.

- "Most people won't realize that writing is a craft." Katherine Anne Porter's words could be the fifth unit's title. Unit 5, *Ready-to-Use Revision & Proofreading Activities*, guides the students through the problem areas of writing. Troublesome areas such as verb tense, words often confused, superfluity, double negatives, and clarity issues are presented in interesting and innovative ways. Students will become better proofreaders as they learn to utilize the same methods used by professional writers.

- "Our appreciation of fine writing will always be in proportion to its real difficulty and its apparent ease." Charles Caleb Colton must have been listening in as Unit 6, *Ready-to-Use Portfolio Development Activities*, was developed. Students are exposed to many different types of practical writings including literary analyses, original stories and sketches, narratives, reviews, letters, journal entries, newspaper articles, character analyses, dialogue writing, college admission essays, and commercials. The goal is to make the difficult appear easy!

Whether you use these realistic classroom-tested activities for introduction, remediation, reinforcement, or enrichment, they will guide your students toward more effective writing. Many of the activities include riddles, hidden words and sayings, word-finds, and other devices that allow students to check their own answers. These activities will also help you to assess your students' progress.

So go ahead and make Mr. Faulkner proud by awakening the experience, observation, and imagination of your students. The benefits will be both theirs—and yours!

Jack Umstatter

ABOUT UNIT 4

For some students the most difficult aspect of a writing assignment is getting started. Whether it is selecting a topic, finding convincing supportive evidence, or organizing the writing, the writing preliminaries can be troublesome. The 90 reproducible activities in *Ready-to-Use Prewriting & Organization Activities*, the *Writing Skills Curriculum Library*'s fourth unit, are designed to make this writing process more enjoyable and less worrisome for your students. These activities guide students through the basics of preparing an effective writing. The benefits are many.

- Activities 1–16 in Section One, "Approaching a Subject," focus on selecting appropriate writing topics. Through several personal inventories, students will focus on their topic preferences. Here students will also brainstorm and respond freely to several directed topics. Finally, important writing terms will be introduced through two fun activities.

- Section Two's activities 17–31, "Research," concentrate on the tools and methodologies of effective research. Since students will become very familiar with printed, visual, and audio reference sources, they will no longer find the library either boring or intimidating! Not only will your students enjoy the challenges of locating specific pieces of information, they will also understand how to organize their findings more efficiently and effectively.

- In Section Three, "Topics and Topic Sentences," activities 32–47 will help students improve their brainstorming skills to select appropriate topics and convincing pieces of evidence. Thesis statements and topic sentences are also covered in this section. Students will become more skillful and knowledgeable in selecting and organizing a topic and its supporting evidence.

- Activities 48–61 in "Organizing," the fourth section, concentrate on grouping ideas, organizing concepts, and outlining the composition or essay. Here, students will become familiar with graphic organizers and other ways of effectively organizing materials. Fun activities include writing directions and composing stories.

- Section Five, "Skills," features activities 62–75, fourteen activities that cover a wide range of writing skills. Diction and syntax activities are found here. Students will also work on word specifics, details, paraphrasing, description, and other writing strategies.

- "Types of Writing," activities 76–90, features many different types of writings. Personal writings, sensory writings, and creative writings will spark your students' interests. Also, specific formats of writing, such as description, process, persuasive, and comparison–contrast, are found in this concluding section.

Your students will become more confident and skilled writers after completing these activities. Plus, they will enjoy themselves and look forward to expressing their thoughts and feelings. Now, that's the right (*and write*) combination!

Jack Umstatter

CONTENTS

SECTION ONE
APPROACHING A SUBJECT

SECTION TWO
RESEARCH

SECTION THREE
TOPICS AND TOPIC SENTENCES

SECTION FOUR
ORGANIZING

SECTION FIVE
SKILLS

SECTION SIX
TYPES OF WRITING

TEACHER'S CORRECTION MARKS

ab	abbreviation problem	pr ref	pronoun reference problem
agr	agreement problem	pun	punctuation needed or missing
amb	ambiguous	reas	reasoning needs improvement
awk	awkward expression or construction	rep	unnecessary repetition
cap	capitalize	RO	run-on
case	error in case	shift	faulty tense shift
cp	comma problem	sp	incorrect spelling
cs	comma splice	thesis	improve the thesis
d	inappropriate diction	trans	improve the transition
det	details are needed	TX	topic sentence needed (or improved)
dm	dangling modifier	U	usage problem
dn	double negative	UW	unclear wording
frag	fragment	V	variety needed
ital	italics or underline	VAG	vague
lc	use lower case	VE	verb error
mm	misplaced modifier	VT	verb tense problem
num	numbers problem	w	wordy
^	insert	WC	better word choice
¶	new paragraph needed	WM	word missing
‖	faulty parallelism	WW	wrong word
,	insert comma		
pass	misuse of passive voice		

APPROACHING A SUBJECT

4-1. LOOKING WITHIN (AND WITHOUT)

Looking for topics that interest you? Fill out this form to take an inventory of the topics and items that interest you. Refer to these answers when you are searching for an assignment topic.

1. Three issues that I feel strongly about are: _____

   _____

   _____

2. My hobbies include: _____

   _____

3. Three of my more memorable days (for better or for worse) include: _____

   _____

   _____

   _____

4. Some changes I would like to see within the next few years include: _____

   _____

   _____

   _____

5. Some of my ideas about the future are: _____

   _____

   _____

6. Education (or, specifically, my education) has its good and bad points. The good points include: _____

   _____

   _____

   The bad points include: _____

   _____

7. I have met some memorable people in my life. Name some and briefly tell what made them memorable. _____

_____

_____

_____

_____

8. The media influence our daily lives. What are some positive aspects of the media? _____

_____

_____

_____

_____

What are some of the negative aspects? _____

_____

_____

_____

_____

9. Most of us love to either tell or hear a good story. What are some of the better ones I have either heard or told? _____

_____

_____

_____

10. Since the beginning of time, human beings have used description to communicate. Here are some people, places, things, or ideas that I would like to describe.

_____

_____

_____

_____

4-2. SEARCHING FOR THE TOPIC

Finding it hard to think of a topic to write about for the next assignment? Here is a list of mind joggers that may help you to select that elusive topic. On the line next to each mind-jogger phrase, write an appropriate answer. That answer may help you to select an interesting topic.

1. a day you would like to relive _____

2. what a true friend is _____

3. your favorite actor or actress or musician or sports celebrity or . . . _____
_____

4. a job you like or dislike _____

5. a scary moment _____

6. being a parent _____

7. your all-time favorite movie _____

8. favorite (or most detested) fictional character _____

9. food _____

10. tattoos _____

11. a trip to an unfamiliar place _____

12. ceremonies _____

13. winter _____

14. vacations _____

15. orthodontists _____

16. working out _____

17. your first date _____

18. bumper stickers _____

19. holidays _____

20. royalty _____

4-3. WRITING JOGGERS

On the lines provided, complete the writing jogger sentence and then continue writing more about the subject introduced in that sentence. This technique should help you to get over the rough spots when attempting to select a topic to write about in a composition.

1. I will never be able to _____

_____

_____

_____

2. It is a shame that _____

_____

_____

_____

3. If I did not see it myself, I would never have believed it happened. Here is what occurred.

_____

_____

_____

4. The perfect crime would be to _____

_____

_____

_____

5. If I could, I would eliminate _____

because _____

_____

_____

6. I often think about changing places with _____

since _____

_____

_____

4-4. THE TWO-MINUTE DRILL

Football teams run their two-minute drill toward the end of the first or second half of the game. We have our own version of the two-minute drill. On the line next to each topic, write down your thoughts about that topic—all in two minutes! You do not have to write complete sentences; words and phrases will do. This activity will help you narrow down your topic and give you some new ideas about the topic as well.

1. your family _____

_____

_____

_____

2. prejudice _____

_____

_____

_____

3. smoking _____

_____

_____

_____

4. cheating _____

_____

_____

_____

5. inventions _____

_____

_____

_____

6. fads _____

_____

_____

_____

7. shopping malls _____

_____

_____

_____

8. natural disasters _____

_____

_____

_____

9. children's television _____

_____

_____

_____

10. professional athletes _____

_____

_____

_____

4-5. LISTING

Searching for an idea or subject for the next writing? Use the same method as professional writ-ers do—list. Think about an important word related to your assigned writing and then list the ideas that come to mind. Do not worry where you are going with the ideas you list. Let the ideas take you! Perhaps then an idea for that next writing will be found within your list.

On the lines provided, list ideas related to the subject given to you. Compare your ideas with those of your classmates.

FEARS

_____

_____

NEWSPAPERS

_____

_____

AUTOBIOGRAPHIES

_____

_____

BEDROOMS

_____

_____

READING

_____

_____

BABYSITTING

_____

_____

THE "GOOD OLD DAYS "

_____

_____

ADVERTISING

_____

_____

4-6. WE THINK ALIKE (AND DIFFERENTLY)

This activity will attempt to prove two things—we all think alike and we all think differently. Start by brainstorming the first word. Spend three minutes brainstorming and writing only words, not sentences. Then compare your answers with those of a partner. See how many words are on both your list and your partner's list. Then brainstorm the next word. With a different partner, compare your list as you did before. Keep doing the same (brainstorm and then compare with a new partner) with each new word. If your teacher so desires, the class can see what words were popular for each brainstormed word. Maybe some ideas for future writings will emerge!

1. shovel

_____

_____

2. lake

_____

_____

3. relatives

_____

_____

4. passport

_____

_____

5. gloves

_____

_____

6. malls

_____

_____

7. library

_____

_____

8. freedom

_____

_____

4-7. BRAINSTORMING WORD-FIND

As Kate and Jamey brainstormed the topic of acting, they listed the 25 words found in this word-find. Circle the words they listed. These words are listed horizontally, vertically, diagonally, forward, and backward. If Kate and Jamey have done well in their brainstorming, they now can select from this list to come up with many possible writing topics!

```
K F R G Y W H A L T D C W M B R E X T K N C O Q
B A P E C T L T C L P O B N T M W C G T Z Q P W
W B R A V E R Y K T H A L L O W E E N U R S E S
L G R S G A M E J I I S Q P R I Y J I E N K R M
Y S T T V E T O B Q T N P X H T T V F C L T A H
F P Y E Q J A B V I W T G Q I I W A R V S O J R
K R L R U A G N P I L Z E N R B N L U Z T K I K
N B J P I N M O T X N T U N S R Z S S D N G Z V
T V W T Z U B I N S S G S N S J S Z T G A B X D
Z Y J B Z A V T D W Y G F Z T J X Z M V R R Q Q
Z O O S E R N A W C O C K L Q N K D X K U X G B
S P G C S Y G R F R G V K J B K Z S X L A K R Q
Q G W G V R R G F C U N K Q B T N Q C T T C W P
K N L C D L C I L K R X M C P L J W P C S F L J
P Z P C X V Q M Q Y T S L H G B M R R K E D N D
T T W F C D V M C N Z Z Q N H L R D N G R K D N
M T G K G G C I T C N Z X L B F R P X F R L D Q
```

ACTING	FROGS	KITTENS	PAGEANTS	UNITY
BRAVERY	GRADUATION	LIBERTY	QUIZZES	VIOLENCE
CARS	HALLOWEEN	MOVING	RESTAURANTS	WAR
DOLPHINS	IMMIGRATION	NURSES	SURFING	YOGURT
EASTER	JANUARY	OPERA	TRAVEL	ZOOS

4-8. TAKE FOUR

Authors think about many different topics while searching for interesting ideas to explore. They brainstorm their knowledge, feelings, and other ideas concerning the subject. Here you will do the same. This activity should take about twenty minutes since you will "take four" minutes to write whatever comes to mind about each of these five subjects. So go ahead and explore and write your ideas about these subjects on the lines provided. Though you should write complete sentences, do not worry about writing perfectly correct grammar.

Physical education classes _____

_____

_____

_____

_____

_____

E-mail _____

_____

_____

_____

_____

_____

A Monday morning in January _____

_____

_____

_____

_____

_____

Funerals _____

_____

_____

_____

_____

_____

_____

Pets _____

_____

_____

_____

_____

_____

_____

_____

4-9. BRAINSTORMING INTO A COMPOSITION

Often the toughest part of an assignment is coming up with ideas for the writing. Brainstorming is an effective way to generate ideas for developing a topic. Sharing your ideas on a subject with others is sometimes helpful to see other aspects of the topic.

Below are four topics that your group of four will consider. Each group member is responsible for recording the ideas the group generates for one of the four topics. Thus, if the topic were Transportation Problems, the group might come up with related ideas such as safety regulations, accidents (both human and mechanical), escalating costs of operating vehicles, fuel consumption, road conditions and maintenance, and inclement weather situations. If this generating of ideas is done correctly, each topic begins to be narrowed and is then more easily handled as you formulate the thesis for your composition.

On the lines below, record the ideas for one of the general topics in the group assigned to you by your teacher. Consider as many aspects of the topic as time allows. Use the reverse side of this page if needed.

Group One: Celebrities, Compact Discs, Television, Reading

Group Two: College, Your Town, Outdoor Sports, Working Out

Group Three: Teens, Pollution, Food, Smoking

Group Four: Parents, Fears, Animals, Phone Calls

Group Five: Radio, Stereotypes, The 21st Century, Jobs

Group Six: Sports, Religions, Leaders, Law Enforcement

_____

_____

_____

_____

_____

_____

_____

_____

_____

_____

4-10. BRAINSTORMING ... THE START OF THE WRITING PROCESS

Brainstorming, the flow of ideas, will help you to gather ideas for a writing assignment. By brainstorming, you allow your mind to expand so that your ideas will come more easily.

Here are ten topics ready for your brainstorming. List your answers in the spaces provided. Relax and let the ideas come to you!

1. List three things that roll.

   _____

2. Who are three infamous people?

   _____

3. Name three machines that were not around a century ago.

   _____

4. What are three things that excite first graders?

   _____

5. What are three things that are old within a week?

   _____

6. Name three favorite vacation spots **not** in North America.

   _____

7. Name three of your current English teacher's favorite expressions.

   _____

8. Name three professional sports teams whose names are associated with **flight.**

   _____

9. What are three board games?

   _____

10. Name three fun activities for senior citizens.

   _____

4-11. MAKING LISTS

On the lines provided, make a list including the items you should consider if you were asked to brainstorm each topic. Include as many thoughts as you can for each topic. Compare your lists with those of your classmates.

War	*Newspapers*	*Selecting A College*
_____	_____	_____
_____	_____	_____
_____	_____	_____
_____	_____	_____
_____	_____	_____
_____	_____	_____
_____	_____	_____
_____	_____	_____
_____	_____	_____
_____	_____	_____
_____	_____	_____
_____	_____	_____
_____	_____	_____

4-12. COOPERATIVE LISTING OF IDEAS

Five topics are listed below. Working with other members of your class, list some ideas connected to that topic. List as many ideas (words, phrases, and sentences are all acceptable) as you can within the time allowed by your teacher. No logical ordering of ideas is expected at this point. Avoid opinions and keep the ideas connected to the topic. An example is done for you.

> *Example:* **Running for political office:** thinking you can win, getting supporters, getting financial backing, having a political platform, knowing the needs of your constituency, having a campaign slogan, writing speeches, delivering speeches, campaign headquarters, knowing opponents' strengths and weaknesses, getting connected with the media

1. learning how to play a musical instrument: _____

_____

_____

2. weight training: _____

_____

_____

3. owning and operating a small business: _____

_____

_____

4. planning a family vacation: _____

_____

_____

5. owning a pet: _____

_____ _____

_____

4-13. EAVESDROPPING AT THE MALL

Eve—the trusty, gossip columnist—overheard these ten sentences at the mall yesterday. Each one could make an interesting story. On the lines below each sentence, brainstorm at least three possible story ideas engendered by that sentence. You do not have to write complete sentences; instead, let the ideas flow and record them. An example is done for you.

> **One teen girl says to another: "He never told me that!"**
> boyfriend wants to break up . . . girl was fired from her job . . .
> girl is confused about something . . . somebody has lied

Son says to his father: "You don't understand teens."

_____

_____

_____

Mother says to the clerk: "You don't seem to understand what I am saying."

_____

_____

_____

One security guard says to the other: "He's wearing a black leather jacket."

_____

_____

_____

Store owner says to her assistant: "He lied on his application."

_____

_____

_____

Mother asks Father: "Where do I draw the line?"

_____

_____

_____

Upon seeing Santa Claus in the mall, a three-year-old says to her father: "Santa Claus is scary."

_____

_____

_____

Teen asks his girlfriend: "Have you seen that new girl in school?"

_____

_____

_____

One five-year-old says to his twin: "The police were running after the two men."

_____

_____

_____

A mother asks her ten-year-old son: "Is that what you really mean?"

_____

_____

_____

Jewelry clerk says to her customer: "This one is rare."

_____

_____

_____

4-14. SETTING THE TERMS

Twenty-five terms that you will need to know in developing solid writing skills are in this word-find. These words are listed below the puzzle. Circle the words in the word-find on a separate piece of paper, and then, define each one. The words can be found backward, forward, horizontally, diagonally, and vertically.

```
R C G H P G D P F D T N J H Q S J X P N G J S Y
E C W N X R T H G N O W R J G D E O Z V J P T C
F B C L I Z O R W N P S O F H G I L U N E D Y N
L I S T I N G C G N I W O R R A N R E R H X L J
E I R G N M I Z E S C T T G G R V I S C N G E N
C C S C N E D F E S E P I J N A E O S V T A M Y
T L R T Q I T H E G S D W R X I N V Y U F I L R
I U M A E H T N N R M C I S W A T I I D C N N V
N S Y U R N Y F O L B R G T L E O I Z S H O K G
G T H D B Z I X A C J G Z W I Y R G R I I K F G
M E Q I W S G N L R Z H R T G N Y P F W N N F N
C R G E J R B S G Y D I H Z S G G Q H W E G G W
N I S N C F B J B F T S Z Z Y T J P R B B E T N
Y N V C F C D H M I F W W Y T B V Z Z M Z T R K
K G T E G J D G N I D A E R F O O R P M Y D C F
F P D B T M D G J L Q R C Z L P F M K Y M Y W M
B K S C O L L E C T I N G I D E A S B B B J Q L
```

AUDIENCE	EDITING	LISTENING	PREWRITING	REVISING
CLUSTERING	FOCUSING	LISTING	PROCESS	SELECTING
COLLECTING IDEAS	FREE WRITING	NARROWING	PROOFREADING	STYLE
CONTENT	JOURNAL	ORGANIZING	REFLECTING	THESIS
DRAFTING	INVENTORY	PERSONAL WRITING	REFINING	TOPIC

4-15. GETTING THE TERMS DOWN

Twenty-five frequently used writing terms are the answers to these clues. Place the answers in their appropriate spaces. Several letters have been placed for you.

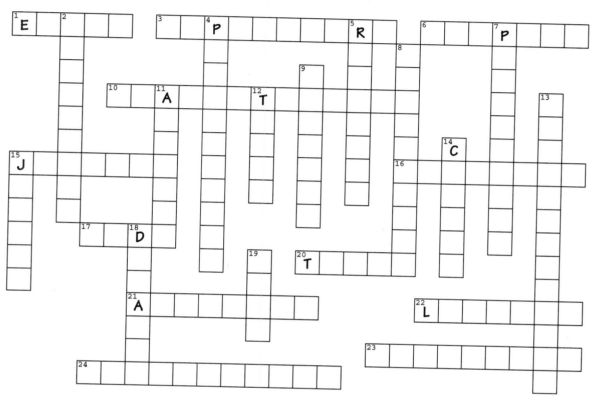

ACROSS

1. prose expressing the author's point of view toward the subject
3. type of writing that explains
6. writer's goal
10. collecting ideas for writing
15. personal record of one's impressions
16. references to a literary or historical person, place, or thing
17. part of the writing between the introduction and the conclusion
20. central idea in a writing
21. people who read the author's writing
22. dictionary definition of the word
23. writing about another's life
24. writing used to describe

DOWN

2. form used by the writer
4. vantage point from which the story is told
5. editing one's writing
7. writing intended to change another's opinion
8. language beyond the dictionary definition
9. necessary steps in developing a piece of writing
11. comparison of two or more similar things
12. specific subject of the writing
13. writing about one's own life
14. overused word or phrase
15. a group's technical language
18. words used to describe, persuade, support, or explain
19. writer's attitude toward the subject

4-16. TALK IT OUT

When a writer is searching for topics and other ideas to write about, he or she will talk about a topic and other ideas with another person. Here you will do much the same, except you will write the "imaginary dialogue" you have with another whom we will call "Him or Her." Start with a topic you introduce and then just, as they say, "go with it." After your dialogue is completed, list possible topics and ideas you discussed or alluded to in your "imaginary dialogue." Use the reverse side if necessary. Have fun!

YOU: _____

_____

HIM OR HER: _____

_____

YOU: _____

_____

HIM OR HER: _____

_____

YOU: _____

_____

HIM OR HER: _____

_____

YOU: _____

_____

HIM OR HER: _____

_____

YOU: _____

_____

HIM OR HER: _____

_____

RESEARCH

4-17. RESEARCH TOOLS

Match the 16 research sources with their definitions. If your answers are correct, the rows, columns, and two diagonals will add up to the same number.

A. Internet	E. Dictionary	I. Encyclopedia	M. Atlas
B. Autobiography	F. Stylebook	J. Review	N. Thesaurus
C. Index	G. Eyewitness account	K. Editorial	O Almanac
D. Biography	H. Anthology	L. Quotations book	P. Diary

1. collection of poems, stories, songs, or the like chosen by the compiler
2. book of maps
3. account of one's own life
4. statement of opinion in a newspaper
5. a critical report of a play, book, performance, or concert
6. alphabetical listing of names and subjects along with their page numbers in a specific text
7. daily written record of one's experiences and thoughts
8. book that alphabetically lists words along with their definitions, pronunciations, etymologies, and more
9. annual publication, usually statistical, on many subjects
10. book consisting of examples or rules of style
11. set of books giving information on many subjects, listed alphabetically
12. account of another person's life
13. telecommunications system featuring web pages
14. direct words on various subjects
15. evidence offered by one who was present at the event
16. book of synonyms and antonyms

A	B	C	D
E	F	G	H
I	J	K	L
M	N	O	P

4-18. RESEARCH MATCHING COLUMN

Match each question with the reference book you would use to find the question's answer. Though an answer may be found in more than one reference book, select the book that most obviously fits. (Each reference book and each question are used only once.) Write the correct letter from Column B on the line next to its match in Column A. If your answers are correct, the letters will spell out (in order) a man's name, a weather condition, a part of a ship, a synonym for strategy, and the initials of the twenty-third U.S. president.

Column A

1. _____ *Animal Life Encyclopedia*

2. _____ *Book Review Index*

3. _____ *Contemporary Authors*

4. _____ *Current Biography*

5. _____ *Education Index*

6. _____ *Encyclopedia of Science and Technology*

7. _____ *Encyclopedia of World Art*

8. _____ *Historic Documents*

9. _____ *Home Book of Quotations*

10. _____ *Mythology of All Races*

11. _____ *Oxford English Dictionary*

12. _____ *Play Index*

13. _____ *Profiles of American Colleges*

14. _____ *Reader's Guide to Periodical Literature*

15. _____ *The Baseball Encyclopedia*

16. _____ *World Atlas*

Column B

A. What majors does Purdue University offer?

B. How many home runs did Mickey Mantle hit in 1961?

C. What are some of Oscar Wilde's more famous quips?

D. Who painted *Christina's World?*

E. What is the last word of the Declaration of Independence?

F. What college did former president George Bush attend?

G. How does a bridge hold its weight?

H. How many miles from Dublin, Ireland is London, England?

I. What did the critics say about the book *The Hunt and the Feast?*

J. How fast can the cheetah run?

K. Who is the Roman god of the sea?

L. Who is the female protagonist in George Bernard Shaw's comedic play *Pygmalion?*

M. How many books has current novelist John Grisham written to date?

N. Where can you find articles about automobile insurance?

O. Why do teachers use cooperative learning?

P. When did the word *numb* first come into the English language?

4-19. IN THE LIBRARY

Writers make valuable use of the library when they research. The answers to the following 15 questions can be found in the local or school library. Try to answer these on your own. If necessary, request the help of a librarian.

1. What is the purpose of a book's call number?_____

   _____

2. Each division of the Dewey Decimal System is divided into how many sections? _____

3. What is the call number of economic books? (a) 090 (b) 330 (c) 760 (d) 870

4. What is the call number of education books? (a) 240 (b) 370 (c) 660 (d) 910

5. Books can be listed in any of three ways within the card catalog. Name these three possible listings. _____

6. Fiction books are organized according to: _____

For questions 7–15, use the information found in this hypothetical *Reader's Guide to Periodical Literature* entry.

MOVIE DIRECTORS
One Man's Band. S. Pond. il Prem 10:100–102 O '96.

7. What is the subject of this entry? _____

8. Who is the author? _____

9. What is the magazine's abbreviation? _____

10. The article is how many pages? _____

11. What does the 10 represent? _____

12. What month is this issue? _____

13. What year was this article published? _____

14. What is the article's title? _____

15. What do the initials *il* stand for? _____

27

4-20. WHICH MAGAZINE?

Knowing his or her sources is important for a detective. The same is true for a writer. Knowing where to locate information helps an author write more informative stories and articles. Match each article title in Column B with its magazine in Column A. Write the two- or three-letter answer on the line next to the number. (Each magazine and each title are used only once.) If your answers are correct, the letters will spell out the names of three other magazines. Write their names on the lines.

Column A

1. _____ Advertising Age
2. _____ Astronomy
3. _____ Boating
4. _____ Business Week
5. _____ Computer World

6. _____ Current Health
7. _____ Education Digest
8. _____ Entertainment Weekly
9. _____ Family Circle
10. _____ Games
11. _____ Hockey News
12. _____ Money
13. _____ New York Review of Books
14. _____ Poetry
15. _____ Popular Science
16. _____ Road and Track
17. _____ Runner's World
18. _____ Seventeen
19. _____ Time

20. _____ Writer's Digest

Column B

AD. "How Many Planets Are There?"

AEO. "Is He the Right Guy for You?"

AR. "Smith Wins the Indianapolis 500"

AT. "New Shakespeare Sonnets Found"

CH. "Record Number Run the New York City Marathon"

ED. "Genes Seen as Contributing Factor"

ER. "Sailing in the Mediterranean"

ES. "Are You Eating the Right Foods?"

GY. "Short Story Writers Find Alternative Styles"

IG. "The Changing World of PCs"

LL. "NHL Looking to Expand Again"

LO. "People Making This Week's News"

PO. "Harrison Ford Signs for Next Movie"

RE. "Super Bowl Commercials Make the Grade"

RT. "Vacations for the Whole Family"

SD. "Companies' Profits Soar"

SI. "Crossword Puzzlers Meet in Toronto"

TR. "Grisham's Book Is Another Thriller"

TS. "Teachers See Additional Problems with Testing"

US. "Mutual Funds and Their Selling Points"

The three magazines are: _____

4-21. MATCHING THE TITLE AND THE FIRST LINE

Match the title and first line from the abstracts (summaries) of the following six magazine articles. Write the correct first line's letter in the space next to its matching number. On the lines following the matching column, write why you matched the title with that particular first line.

Titles

1. _____ "Changing Gracefully"
2. _____ "No Wave Is Insignificant"
3. _____ "On the Double"
4. _____ "The $10 Face"

5. _____ "Braving the Elements"
6. _____ "The Biting Truth"
7. _____ "The Thin White Line"
8. _____ "Calling It Quits"

First Lines

A. Several programs are available to help teens stop smoking.

B. Voice dubbing has been common throughout the history of musical films.

C. . . . and his family run an instructional camp for surfing . . .

D. Makeup need not be expensive.

E. Examining teeth can help hunters identify animal skulls found in the wild.

F. The federal government has charged six U.S. lawyers with cocaine trafficking instead of obstruction of justice for their misconduct and involvement with defendants in drug cases.

G. Driving in poor weather is difficult and can cause drivers to be more stressed.

H. Desktop publishers need to take the entire workflow process into account when they implement changes.

Reasons

1. _____
2. _____
3. _____
4. _____
5. _____
6. _____
7. _____
8. _____

4-22. WHICH SOURCE?

Knowing where to locate needed information is essential for any good writer. On the line next to each needed fact, write the letter that corresponds to one of the five sources. Some may have more than one answer.

(A) dictionary; **(B)** encyclopedia; **(C)** atlas; **(D)** biography; **(E)** almanac

1. _____ China's population

2. _____ number of miles of rivers in China

3. _____ synonym for the word *grave*

4. _____ birthplace of Pierre Trudeau

5. _____ Virginia colleges

6. _____ Sir Elton John's age

7. _____ college attended by former President Jimmy Carter

8. _____ correct pronunciation of the word *orange*

9. _____ the names of the six New England States

10. _____ Hillary Clinton's maiden name

11. _____ number of inches of rain in New Jersey last year

12. _____ temperature at which water boils

13. _____ African deserts

14. _____ The Beatles' first number-one hit

15. _____ the artist Michelangelo's last name

4-23. YOU CAN FIND IT

The following 15 questions need answers. Using various printed reference sources, write each answer and the source that contains the answer. An example is done for you.

Example: How is botulism spread? Botulism is spread by consuming contaminated foods. *The New York Public Library Desk Reference*

1. Describe a ciseaux in ballet. _____
   _____

2. Approximately how many hours are needed to roast an eight-pound turkey? _____
   _____

3. Which of the constellations is the Archer? _____
   _____

4. Which professional football team won the 1974 Super Bowl? _____
   _____

5. What is a Druze? _____
   _____

6. Kampala is the capital of what country? _____
   _____

7. In what Canadian city is the Professional Hockey Hall of Fame located? _____
   _____

8. What does the Spanish word *campesino* mean? _____
   _____

9. What did Andre Jacques Garnerin invent in 1797? _____
   _____

10. Which Italian artist sculpted *Perseus with the Head of Medusa*? _____
    _____

11. Which author's pseudonym is Eric Arthur Blair? _____
    _____

12. What is the term used to describe the main character in a story or play? _____
    _____

13. Who was reappointed as the United States's Poet Laureate in April 1999? _____
    _____

14. In what year was James Urmson's *A Concise Encyclopedia of Western Philosophy and Philoso-phers* published? _____

15. In what year did the U.S. Supreme Court decide on the *Roe vs. Wade* case? _____
    _____

4-24. LOCATING INFORMATION

Like good detectives, writers have their favorite sources. Knowing where to obtain information is important for any writer. Without it, you might not have an interesting story. With it, you have the making of an intelligent, interesting, and informative piece of writing. Knowledge is power!

For each task below, list at least three sources for finding the necessary information. Which books, people, and places would you use? Be as specific as you can. The encyclopedia or the internet are acceptable sources, but look for others as well. Write your answers on the lines provided.

1. Your family tree _____

2. The causes of the war in Vietnam _____

3. The problems with the ozone layer _____

4. Information about Manhattan College _____

5. The life of Richard M. Nixon _____

6. The Greenpeace Foundation (environmental organization) _____

7. Techniques of Paleolithic cave paintings _____

8. The political satire of *Newsday* cartoonist Doug Marlette _____

9. The sun as a symbol in mythology _____

10. The life and works of musician Eric Clapton _____

11. The 1906 San Francisco Earthquake _____

12. The Australian educational system _____

13. The role of newspapers in a democratic society _____

14. The facts surrounding the Attica Prison riots _____

15. The effectiveness of herbs on health _____

4-25. WHERE CAN YOU FIND IT?

Good writers know where to search for information. Whether you are writing an essay or a term paper, you will need to know where to locate information. Using any resource in print, find the answer to each question. Then, on the lines provided, write each answer and its specific source. An example is done for you.

> **Example :** *Which movie won the Oscar® for Best Picture in 1996? Braveheart; Speaking Freely*

1. The prefix "ped-" refers to what body part? _____

2. Which astronaut said, "That's one small step for a man, one giant leap for mankind," on July 20, 1969? _____

3. What is the nickname for the teams at Howard University in Washington, DC?

   _____

4. What American woman organized the American Red Cross in 1881? _____

5. Which scientist discovered hydrogen? _____

6. When did American poet Robert Frost die? _____

7. Who colonized Greenland in A.D. 985? _____

8. Which Secretary of the Treasury had the initials "S.C."? _____

9. What is the highest point in the state of Kansas? _____

10. What author created the detective Philip Marlowe? _____

11. In chemistry, what do the letters of the acronym "A.M.U." represent? _____

12. What is the capital city of Portugal? _____

13. What is the name of Hamlet's girlfriend? _____

14. In what New York town is the Baseball Hall of Fame located? _____

15. Fill in the last word of this song by Roberta Flack: *Killing Me* _____

4-26. LET'S GO AND FIND IT

Using the correct sources, write the answer to each question on the line provided.

1. What is Gwent? _____

2. What is Habima? _____

3. Who was Hadrian? _____

4. What is a hagiography? _____

5. Who was Haile Selassie? _____

6. Who was George Halas? _____

7. Who was Edmund Halley? _____

8. Who is Paul Newman? _____

9. Who was Aloysius Gonzaga? _____

10. What does the Gordian knot symbolize? _____

11. Who was Grant Wood? _____

12. Who is Bruce Jenner? _____

13. Who was William Wordsworth? _____

14. Where is Ulysses S. Grant buried? _____

15. Shirley Grau's Pulitzer Prize novel is entitled *The* _____ *of the House.*

16. Greasewood is a(n) _____

17. What is *The Great Train Robbery?* _____

18. What is the monetary unit of Greece? _____

19. In what Canadian province was retired hockey star Wayne Gretzky born? _____

20. Where are the Grampian Mountains located? _____

4-27. FINDING THE ANSWERS

The following 15 questions need to be answered. Research these questions. Write the answers on the first line. Then, on the second line, cite the resource used to find the answer.

1. What has been the most popular name for the Pope? (a) John (b) Pius (c) Paul (d) Gregory

   Answer: _____

   Source: _____

2. By what more familiar names are Robert Leroy Parker and Harry Longbaugh known?

   Answer: _____

   Source: _____

3. A fathom is how many feet?

   Answer: _____

   Source: _____

4. With what religion is the menorah associated?

   Answer: _____

   Source: _____

5. What is the real name of former U.S. President Gerald Ford?

   Answer: _____

   Source: _____

6. Which U.S. President served only 31 days in office?

   Answer: _____

   Source: _____

7. What British novel begins with this line," It was the best of times, it was the worst of times . . ."?

   Answer: _____

   Source: _____

8. How many years was the Hundred Years War?

   Answer: _____

   Source: _____

9. June 6, 1944 is better known by what other name?

   Answer: _____

   Source: _____

10. In what American city was Tin Pan Alley?

    Answer: _____

    Source: _____

11. What liquid is also the same name as Eric Clapton's former musical group?

    Answer: _____

    Source: _____

12. In which sport do the players use a shuttlecock?

    Answer: _____

    Source: _____

13. With what body part is tinnitus associated?

    Answer: _____

    Source: _____

14. In what Canadian province is Lake Louise?

    Answer: _____

    Source: _____

15. Which is the correct spelling? (a) khakie (b) kahki (c) kakhi (d) khaki

    Answer: _____

    Source: _____

4-28. "RESEARCHING THE ANSWERS" CONTEST

How good a researcher are you? Here are 20 questions that need answers. Use whatever sources you need to find these answers. Write your answers on the lines provided. Next to each answer, write the name of the book you used to find the answer.

1. What do the letters SCUBA stand for? _____

2. What artist painted "The Passion of Sacco and Vanzetti"? _____

3. What is a sampan? _____

4. Who was Poland's first winner of the Nobel Prize in Literature? _____

5. What country is directly south of Detroit, Michigan? _____

6. What treaty was signed on December 24, 1814? _____

7. Who won the U.S. Women's Open Golf Championship in 1992? _____

8. What do the initials GRE stand for? _____

9. In what year was the University of Calcutta (India) founded? _____

10. An American feminist born in 1818 and the author of *Sailor on Horseback* share what same last name? _____

11. What was the 1991 sequel to Margaret Mitchell's *Gone With the Wind*? _____

12. What country owns the famous Rock of Gibraltar? _____

13. What is the westernmost Canadian province? _____

14. Who betrayed Jesus Christ? _____

15. What famous American jazz singer was born on April 25, 1918, and died on June 15, 1996? _____

16. What play was Abraham Lincoln watching when he was killed on April 14, 1865? _____

17. After the Diet of Worms (1521) placed Martin Luther under an imperial ban, what Saxon ruler took him into custody? _____

18. Who was the Norse goddess of love and beauty? _____

19. In what sport did the trio of Joe Tinker, John Evers, and Frank Chance gain their fame? _____

20. The actor/comedian Jerry Seinfeld attended what high school on Long Island, New York? _____

4-29. DICTIONARY MAGIC SQUARE

Using a dictionary is a valuable skill for any writer. Whether it is to check on a word's meaning or part of speech or connotation, the good writer knows how to use the dictionary. You will do the same today. Your task, however, is to research the origin or derivation of the 16 words listed below. Match the word with its derivation by placing the proper letter in the correct square. If your answers are correct, with horizontal, vertical, and diagonal rows add up to the same number. Good luck!

A. malapropism	E. mimic	I. mystery	M. posse
B. sandwich	F. clue	J. alimony	N. posh
C. tomato	G. anthology	K. salary	O. profanity
D. assassin	H. bedlam	L. bandit	P. ink

1. ball of thread
2. divine secret
3. outside the temple
4. drug fiend
5. power of the county
6. a card game request
7. London insane asylum
8. money for salt

9. love apple
10. burn
11. eating money
12. actor
13. under summons
14. bouquet of flowers
15. a female character
16. ship's berth

A	B	C	D
E	F	G	H
I	J	K	L
M	N	O	P

4-30. THE 5 W'S AND THE 1 H

The 5 W's and the 1 H (Who? What? Where? When? Why? and How?) will help you to select information about your subject. A sample regarding Shakespeare's *Romeo and Juliet* is below. Read this and, then, on a separate sheet of paper, do the same for two other topics you choose from a list suggested by your teacher. As in the Shakespearean example, the answers do not have to be written in complete sentences.

TOPIC: Shakespeare's *Romeo and Juliet*

Who? Major characters include Romeo Montague, Juliet Capulet, Friar Laurence, and the Nurse

What? Romeo meets and falls immediately in love with Juliet at her family's ball. The Montagues and Capulets have been feuding for years. Friar Laurence secretly marries the two. Romeo is banished for killing Tybalt, Juliet's cousin. Juliet, wanting to be with Romeo and not wanting to marry Paris as her parents so desire, takes a sleeping potion under Friar Laurence's direction. This potion will give her the appearance of death for 42 hours. Unfortunately, the message from Friar Laurence to Romeo (about this sleeping potion plan) never reaches Romeo in Mantua where he is hiding out. Thinking Juliet dead (as she appears in her family's crypt), Romeo drinks poison. Juliet awakens, sees Romeo dead, stabs herself, and dies. The feuding families finally make peace.

Where? Verona and Mantua

When? Original historical setting is about 1303

Why? Because of the feud, the two teenagers had to conceal their love and actions from most others. This eventually leads to both deaths and the subsequent peace.

How? Much of this is covered in What? and Why?

4-31. YOUR NOTE CARDS

How you gather and organize the materials you need for your report or longer paper is important. Keeping note cards is a logical and orderly method of keeping track of your research finding. Hypothetically, you will do a report on an author's life. First, select an author. Then find some information about the author's life. Using the guidelines shown on each card below, fill in the necessary information about your author on a 4″ × 6″ index card.

1 - descriptive heading	2 - number
	you assign to
	the source
5 - subtopic	of information
4 - supporting detail	
3 - cited information (including page number)	

(1) This is a descriptive heading of the information you will cite in #3. Thus, if the information is a quote about the author's formal education, the descriptive heading could be *high school embarrassment.*

(2) Assign each different source you use—each book, each magazine, each Internet location, each interview, etc.—a source number. If you use two articles from the same magazine, assign each magazine the same source number.

(3) In this area you will summarize, paraphrase, or quote directly the information you found in the source you have used (and noted in #2 above). Be sure to note the difference between a direct quote and a paraphrase. The quote could be *"Johnson felt embarrassed by how much he did not know in high school. In some classes, his grades were quite low."* Include the source's page number.

(4) Here you will write a supporting detail of the subtopic you use in #5 below. If the subtopic is *"high school education,"* for example, a supporting detail might be *"poor grades in h.s."*

(5) This is the subtopic of your topic. Considering the information found in # 1–4 above, *"high school education"* might be an appropriate subtopic.

TOPICS AND TOPIC SENTENCES

4-32. TAKING INVENTORY

Throughout the school year, you will be asked to write about certain topics and issues. This page can serve as an inventory of the topics that interest you. For each letter below, list a topic that interests you. You may list more than one. You do not have to have a topic for each letter (unless xylophones and xenophobia are favorite topics of yours).

A _____   N _____

B _____   O _____

C _____   P _____

D _____   Q _____

E _____   R _____

F _____   S _____

G _____   T _____

H _____   U _____

I _____   V _____

J _____   W _____

K _____   X _____

L _____   Y _____

M _____   Z _____

4-33. SOME IDEAS FOR YOU

Selecting a topic can be somewhat difficult. The following list might help you to choose a workable topic. Circle the topics that interest you. Then keep this list in your notebook or folder and refer to it when you need to come up with an idea for the next writing assignment.

accidents	budgets	death	health	organizations
actors and actresses	business	diets	history	parents
	cartoons	disabilities	holidays	plants
aging	celebrities	disasters	Internet	population
alcohol	children	diseases	language	presidents
aliens	cities of the world	divorce	laws	radio
allergies		drugs	literature	recreational activities
activities	clothing	education	magazines	
animals	colleges	elections	medical professionals	religions
arms control	comics	employment		schools
art	computers	exploration	medicine	science
astronomy	consumers	family	money	sports
authors	countries of the world	foods	music	television
aviation	crime	friends	names	transportation
awards	customs	governments	newspapers	vacations
biology	dance		nutrition	war
				weather

4-34. TAKING A CLOSER LOOK AT YOURSELF

Examining your life—including the people, places, things, events, and ideas that make you special—is a good way to develop writing topics. On the lines following each topic, list your appropriate examples. Later, these examples can be used as topics for your compositions and stories.

Admirable people: _____

Unique people: _____

Controversial people: _____

Interesting places: _____

Beautiful places: _____

Memorable places: _____

Favorite possessions: _____

Important personal achievements: _____

Scary experiences: _____

Important activities: _____

Memorable childhood events: _____

Important relationships: _____

Academic successes: _____

Teams, clubs, and other organizations: _____

Musical interests/memories: _____

Funny moments: _____

Sad moments: _____

4-35. FINDING THE 26 TOPICS FROM A TO Z

Twenty-six topics are hidden in this word-find puzzle. Since each topic begins with a different letter, all 26 letters of the alphabet are used. Circle the words—written forward, backward, vertically, or horizontally, or diagonally—and then think of various subtopics for each larger topic.

```
R Z T P Z W Z Y L B Q M Q L H D P Q G X G D W F
C F R H U G O C N O P Y B B R S R W S P J H F P
L I A M E N E R G Y N X S O O Z V I O L E N C E
Y L V F V I I M R H O E F L Y A Y T O E C A A P
F G E U C P T O L I K U L W A J T V R A E V R J
H N L R N P G J N O E D T I W M F S A S E I S M
S P O N R O Q J J S X S E H N Y I S G U R G B N
V T C I E H B U H W Q E Y S L E E N N R G A W V
M F C T T S J N O B V K N T S P S Z A E V T P W
X T U U I A L S N T M R F O O E K S K Q H I M Q
W S P R R B R F N X A L C C P K R F Q X W O D G
T J A E E F Q G T R L T S V P H J T G B G N C N
V V T X M C Z L I T W O I B J P O V S H D T S H
P H I M E D S S W M R P Y O V G X B W L N Y Q G
C M O S N J W X W O M F H Z N C R S I P X T K K
N P N G T Y T R H G W I K Y S S W D Z A D N R Y
H T S C C F Q C Q V L Z H B T S N Q H X Q P J K
```

ANIMALS	GREECE	MAIL	TRAVEL
BOATS	HOROSCOPES	NAVIGATION	UNIONS
CARS	IMMIGRATION	OCCUPATIONS	VIOLENCE
DESSERTS	JOKES	PLEASURE	WORRIES
ENERGY	KANGAROOS	QUOTATIONS	XENOPHOBIA
FURNITURE	LONELINESS	RETIREMENT	YOUTH
		SHOPPING	ZOOS

4-36. TWENTY-FIVE HIDDEN TOPICS

Twenty-five topics are hidden in this word-find. Circle the topic and then, on a separate sheet of paper, write a thesis statement about each one. For example, when you find the topic "Dancing," an appropriate thesis statement might be "Dancing is an exhilarating activity." Good luck!

```
R Q W F P G V Y Y F L Y D G S Y W C F Y F D S Z
A C D R Q B V R M K C X L M Y I S G S B O R U B
D T T I S X S Y H W X D N G N G D N K H O E N G
I V F E C N A R F M A R A T H O N S Y T T S G G
O X P N L G O W E N N L E F X H U I S H W S L N
V A C D G E T I C T K R K P N G O M C E E E A Y
T K O S Y T P I T K U C F I H H R U R A A S S G
B P N H M R N H J A X P J V N I G S A T R S S F
A H C I N G C K O E R F M L M G Y I P E I D E D
S V E P A Y B T B N W E X O T H A C E R A V S D
E Z R G S S B W T V E E P K C W L Y R L H D F W
B C T G T L F F V R Q S L O W A P R S B P B B D
A Y S R I P M L F G J V T R S Y R T P Z W N P S
L D M J C S Y P T B Q M P X Y S D S R T J R X C
L Z B R S J J R S C P G G L W J S J P F C Z J H
Z G S W D B X B W T N H H Z V G D V K J J F D J
G F L F K M D K L G C G T Q M F X M X W K C X C
```

BASEBALL	FOOTWEAR	HIGHWAYS	PLAYGROUNDS	TAPES
COMPUTERS	FRANCE	JEWELRY	RACING	TELEPHONES
CONCERTS	FRIENDSHIP	MARATHONS	RADIO	THEATER
DANCING	GYMNASTICS	MUSIC	SKYSCRAPERS	WALKING
DRESSES	HAIR	OPERATIONS	SUNGLASSES	WINTER

Name _____ Date _____ Period _____

4-37. TAKE FIVE MINUTES

Writers must decide what they are going to write about. Selecting a topic is a major hurdle. Selecting what to write about that topic is often as difficult. How do you make that selection? This activity will help you to select topics and details of that topic more effectively.

Four topics are listed below. For each topic write freely and rapidly for five minutes. Do not write sentences! As you write in this fragmented way, ideas for your topic should come to mind. Even though the topic might not be high on your interest list, write about it anyway. Who knows what might happen?

Dreams _____

_____

_____

_____

_____

Computer Games _____

_____

_____

_____

_____

Relatives _____

_____

_____

_____

_____

Music _____

_____

_____

_____

_____

4-38. LETTING YOUR MIND WANDER

For each of these five topics, write as many ideas as you can within the three minutes allowed by your teacher. Then compare your ideas with those of your classmates. There are no specific correct answers. An example of one topic is done for you. Have fun!

Example topic: **THE COMPUTER** *learning how to use it, printer, paper, monitor, Internet, cost, maintenance, Web pages, e-mail, laser, discs, research, term papers, starting up, privacy, chat rooms, typing, problems*

1. MUSIC _____

_____

_____

2. FRIENDSHIP _____

_____

_____

3. DENTISTS _____

_____

_____

4. SUMMER _____

_____

_____

5. READING _____

_____

_____

4-39. QUESTIONS

When writing about a topic, it is wise to brainstorm that topic. In brainstorming, the writer jots down ideas and questions about the topic. In this way the writer will move along the path to a successful composition.

The topic is computers. Here is a list of subtopic ideas that came to the writer. On the lines next to each subtopic, write two questions that come to mind about that aspect of the bigger topic—computers. The first subtopic's questions are given for you.

assessing your computer needs: <u>"What will I need this computer to do for me?" "How advanced</u>

<u>a computer will I need?"</u> _____

comparing computers: _____

_____

purchasing a computer: _____

_____

installing a computer: _____

_____

operating a computer: _____

_____

selecting computer programs: _____

_____

maintaining a computer: _____

_____

repairing a computer: _____

_____

upgrading a computer: _____

_____

4-40. TOPIC, SUBTOPICS, AND FACTS

Each of the following 20 facts about Ireland, the topic of this activity, has been assigned a number. These facts (in notes form and not complete sentences) are taken from five subtopics. Assign a name to each subtopic and write the five numbers that belong under that subtopic. Each subtopic has four facts. Write your answers in the appropriate spaces below the 20 facts.

1. majority of the population . . . Roman Catholic
2. 1167—King Henry invaded
3. currency unit = pound
4. member of the United Nations and other governmental organizations
5. climate greatly influenced by maritime
6. prime minister heads House of Representatives
7. heavily dependent on foreign oil
8. other religions . . . Protestant and Anglican
9. 2,200 years ago—Celts invaded and divided country into smaller kingdoms
10. more than one-third of Ireland is moor or heath
11. high humidity
12. culturally homogeneous residents
13. diversified economy with agriculture and manufacturing
14. Vikings raided in 800s
15. president in office for seven years
16. English universally spoken
17. 1845—potato famine
18. republic form of government
19. mining increasing
20. many lakes, marshes, and peat bogs

Subtopic   **Facts (numbers)**

_____   _____

_____   _____

_____   _____

_____   _____

_____   _____

4-41. SUPPORTING THE TOPIC

For each thesis statement below, list three specific supporting points. If you disagree with the thesis statement, reword it, and then offer three supporting points for your view on the topic. An example is given to you.

English is my favorite subject.

(a) We read interesting novels, stories, plays, and poems.

(b) We discuss our feelings about the characters and the topics found in our readings.

(c) I enjoy writing and sharing my ideas with other students.

1. **Summer is the best season of the year.**

(a) _____

_____

(b) _____

_____

(c) _____

_____

2. **Cigarettes should not be sold to minors.**

(a) _____

_____

(b) _____

_____

(c) _____

_____

3. **Professional athletes are role models.**

(a) _____

_____

(b) _____

_____

(c) _____

_____

4-41. SUPPORTING THE TOPIC (cont'd)

4. Clothes define a person.

   (a) _____

   _____

   (b) _____

   _____

   (c) _____

   _____

5. The death penalty is too harsh a penalty.

   (a) _____

   _____

   (b) _____

   _____

   (c) _____

   _____

6. Teens deal with too much pressure.

   (a) _____

   _____

   (b) _____

   _____

   (c) _____

   _____

7. Computers play too important a role in our society.

   (a) _____

   _____

   (b) _____

   _____

   (c) _____

   _____

8. Our government should spend more money on _____. (Name a problem.)

   (a) _____

   _____

   (b) _____

   _____

   (c) _____

   _____

4-42. WHAT TO INCLUDE

Suppose you had to write a report on each of the following topics. What subtopics would you include? Why? For each of these topics, list at least three subtopics. Some topics are very broad while some are more focused. Discuss your answers with your classmates. An example is done for you.

Topic	Subtopics
Any country of the world . . .	people, principal cities, land, climate, economy

1. Literature . . . _____
   _____

2. The school dropout . . . . _____
   _____

3. The turmoil of the 1960s . . . _____
   _____

4. How to study for an exam . . . _____
   _____

5. The road to better physical health . . . _____
   _____

6. Getting published . . . _____
   _____

7. Taking better photographs . . . _____
   _____

8. Selecting the right college . . . _____
   _____

9. Friendship . . . _____
   _____

10. Vocabulary development . . . _____
    _____

4-43. CONSTRUCTING EFFECTIVE TOPIC SENTENCES

The topic sentence, usually the first or one of the first sentences in the paragraph, states the paragraph's topic. Clear and concise, the topic sentence also gives the author's impression concerning the subject. To maintain unity, the sentences that follow the topic sentence must be related to the topic sentence.

Revise the following 15 ineffective topic sentences, making sure you limit the topic and give a specific impression. Write the improved topic sentences on the appropriate lines. An example is given to you.

> The lecture was presented by Professor Tynan.
>
> Professor Tynan's lecture was both stimulating and entertaining.

1. My father is a carpenter.

   _____

   _____

2. School academics can be tough.

   _____

   _____

3. We need to improve the sleeping accommodations of this camp.

   _____

   _____

4. A friend is that person on whom you can count.

   _____

   _____

5. Los Angeles is a city on the western coast of the United States.

   _____

   _____

6. Rome is a city tourists go to.

   _____

   _____

7. The graduation ceremony took place last Saturday.

_____

_____

8. Martina takes many photographs for our yearbook.

_____

_____

9. Newspaper reporting has changed in the last fifty years.

_____

_____

10. Parents object to some television programs their children watch.

_____

_____

11. Coach Geiger has angered people.

_____

_____

12. Many college students have to take Composition 101.

_____

_____

13. Our club has leaders.

_____

_____

14. We have an opinion about that movie.

_____

_____

15. This sentence is about running.

_____

_____

4-44. OPENING LINES OF MAGAZINE ARTICLES

Four opening portions of magazine articles appear below. On the lines after these openers, write your answers to these three questions: (1) What is the article's topic? (2) What is the author's thesis? (3) What do you think the rest of the article's content will be? Discuss your answers with your classmates.

A. The more I, as a clergyman, have dealt with people's problems and the more I have looked at my own life honestly, the more concerned I am that a lot of misery can be traced to one mistaken notion: we need to be perfect for people to love us. (HAROLD S. KUSHNER, "HOW GOOD DO WE HAVE TO BE?" FROM READER'S DIGEST, MAY 1997, PAGE 163)

1. _____

_____

2. _____

_____

3. _____

_____

B. Meteors and comets have struck Earth repeatedly. One may have wiped out the dinosaurs 65 million years ago. The big question, of course, is when will the next one hit? (JEFFREY WINTERS, "THE NOVEMBER NEMESIS" FROM DISCOVER, AUGUST 1997, PAGE 28)

1. _____

_____

2. _____

_____

3. _____

_____

C. Europe and Asia may seem worlds away, but with our increasingly global economy, other continents are getting closer and closer—at least as far as trade is concerned. (SCHOLASTIC UPDATE, MARCH 7, 1997 PAGE 12)

1. _____

   _____

2. _____

   _____

3. _____

   _____

D. White-collar criminals do not really deserve to go to jail. Prison is expensive and, for such criminals, serves no useful purpose. ("THE WHITE-COLLAR CRIMINAL'S SURVIVAL GUIDE," EXCERPTED FROM DOING FEDERAL TIME: A HANDBOOK FOR BUSINESSMEN WHO ARE FACING FEDERAL WHITE-COLLAR CRIME CHARGES BY RONALD TERMEER IN HARPER'S MAGAZINE, JULY 1997, PAGE 19)

1. _____

   _____

2. _____

   _____

3. _____

   _____

4-45. RECOGNIZING A THESIS STATEMENT

A good thesis statement introduces the topic, states the writer's opinion, and forces the writer to persuade the reader that this statement of opinion is valid. The thesis statement is really a purpose statement. For each of the following thesis statements, circle the writer's specific topic and underline the writer's opinion.

1. Our last summer vacation was a difficult time for all of us.

2. Mr. Kendall's English class is a test of my patience.

3. The 1980s was a controversial decade.

4. Michael Jordan's retirement was a time of mixed emotions for many sports fans.

5. Jay Leno is America's premier comedian.

6. My first year at the new school was very emotional.

7. Lara Thomas was the biggest influence in my dancing career.

8. There is no reason why the senior class members cannot enjoy off-campus privileges.

9. Eating healthy foods is a major contributor to one's fitness.

10. Capital punishment should be eliminated.

11. My mother is the sweetest woman in the world.

12. This activity is not that difficult.

13. Chicago winters are a challenge to all commuters.

14. My Toyota Camry is a joy to own.

15. This is the messiest room I have ever seen.

16. The Quit Smoking program is an unparalleled success.

17. Andrew Lloyd Webber has composed some of the world's most beautiful songs.

18. This movie was not worth the price of admission!

19. The *Oxford English Dictionary* is a great language resource.

4-46. IMPROVING THESIS STATEMENTS

Keeping in mind that a thesis statement introduces a specific topic, states the author's opinion, and is limited and clear in its content, improve these 15 thesis statements. Is the topic limited enough? Is the opinion clearly stated? Is the sentence a fact or is it an opinion that could be challenged? If it can be challenged, if it has a limited subject, and if the opinion is clear, then you have a good thesis statement. Write the revised thesis statement on the lines provided.

1. *Romeo and Juliet* is a play by Shakespeare. _____

2. This essay will show my opinion about cheating on school exams. _____

3. My younger sister is an interesting type of person. _____

4. There are many reasons why I feel that way concerning Jake's statement. _____

5. I have three cats at home. _____

6. This is a good company to work for. _____

7. These two poems are very different. _____

8. Of all the pizza places in town, we usually go to Vinnie's. _____

9. This class can be better. _____

10. Some radio stations are not my cup of tea. _____

11. They would never live in that neighborhood again. _____

12. Our government needs to act now. _____

13. Reading has its good points. _____

14. The movie is different. _____

15. *M*A*S*H* was a good television show. _____

4-47. FLIPPING THROUGH
FOR THE NEXT WRITING

Need ideas for the next writing? Here's a suggestion. Flip through newspapers and magazines looking at their stories' headlines. If you are interested in the story, read it! Information contained within the article may spark an idea that leads to a writing. You never know!

Read the eight headlines below. Then, on the appropriate lines, write at least three ideas that came to you and that could be used for future writings. Your ideas can be in note form instead of complete sentences. Share your ideas with your classmates.

1. "Musicians Honored at City Hall" _____

_____

_____

2. "Top Internet Companies Seek Merger" _____

_____

_____

3. "Tapes Show Robbery Taking Place" _____

_____

_____

4. "Consumers Face Higher Fees" _____

_____

_____

5. "34 Million Americans Have Chronic Pain" _____

_____

_____

6. "DNA Sample Crucial to Murder Case" _____

_____

_____

7. "Caspian Sea Could Be One of World's Great Oil Regions" _____

_____

_____

8. "Students Protest Proposed Testing Changes" _____

_____

_____

ORGANIZING

4-48. TO THE MARKET WE GO

Twenty-four items, arranged in alphabetical order, are on the supermarket shopping list. These items should be divided into six 4-item groups according to their location in the supermarket. On the lines provided, write the items in their proper groups and assign the group a name.

apples	hair spray	peaches	pork chops
bananas	milk	peanuts	potato chips
cheese	nail polish	pears	pretzels
chicken	orange juice	plastic forks	roast beef
deodorant	paper cups	plastic knives	steak
eggs	paper napkins	popcorn	toothpaste

Group name: _____   Items: _____

_____

Group name: _____   Items: _____

_____

Group name: _____   Items: _____

_____

Group name: _____   Items: _____

_____

Group name: _____   Items: _____

_____

Group name: _____   Items: _____

_____

4-49. ORGANIZING THE FIVE GROUPS

Twenty-five terms from five different topics are listed below. List the five terms for each topic next to that topic's name at the bottom of the sheet. The first letter of the topic is given to you. Fill in the topic's other letters.

apartment	circuit board	fret	monitor	rhythm
byte	coach's box	igloo	mound	split-level
celestial sphere	concerto	inning	mouse	sunspot
chip	eclipse	mansion	quarter note	tepee
chord	equinox	mitt	quasar	warning track

Group Name   **Terms**

A _ _ _ _ _ _ _ _ _   _____

                         _____

B _ _ _ _ _ _ _ _   _____

                         _____

C _ _ _ _ _ _ _ _   _____

                         _____

H _ _ _ _ _ _   _____

                         _____

M _ _ _ _ _   _____

                         _____

4-50. SORTING THINGS OUT

Classifying is sorting things into groups. When you are asked to differentiate types of music or dress styles or colleges, you will be classifying specific items. Thus, a classification essay is the writer's attempt to separate things into their elements and then group these items based on similarities. To create order and meaning is one of the classification writer's primary goals.

The classification essay breaks the whole into components. Suppose, for example, the assigned topic is *Literature*. The classification process moves from the *General Topic* (Literature) to the *Specific Subject* (Poetry) to the *Category* (War Poetry) and then to the *Details* (specific characteristics of that type of poetry).

Select three topics below. Using the system discussed above, fill in the spaces with your classification ideas. Discuss your answers with your classmates.

Music	Transportation Vehicles	Television Programs
Fast Foods	Hairstyles	Movies
Parents	Bumper Stickers	Academic Subjects
Pets	Responsibilities	Jobs
Newspaper Parts	Sports	Clothing Styles

General Topic: _____

Specific Subject: _____

Category: _____

Details: _____

_____

General Topic: _____

Specific Subject: _____

Category: _____

Details: _____

_____

General Topic: _____

Specific Subject: _____

Category: _____

Details: _____

_____

4-51. MAKING THE CONNECTION

As you brainstorm, your mind is working quite logically (though it might not seem that way!) connecting one idea with another. You will do the same connecting process here. Thus, you will perform a "directed brainstorm." You are given the first word and one or two more in each series of connectors. Moving from left to right and then doing the same on the next line of blanks, fill in each blank that connects (in some logical fashion) to the word preceding it and then to the word directly after it. Write your words in the blanks and be ready to explain your choices. Moving along and connecting ideas is a fine way to gather topics and information for your writings!

1. computer   paper   _____   ink

 _____   _____

2. holidays   _____   presents

 _____   _____   _____

3. bicycles   _____   _____   pedals

 _____   chain   _____   _____

4. radio   music   _____   _____

 _____   _____   cars

5. exams   pressure   exercise   _____

 _____   _____   _____

6. hands   _____   work   _____

 _____   _____   artists   _____

7. airports   snacks   _____   _____

 _____   _____   _____

8. telephone   _____   _____   inventors

 _____   _____   _____   _____

4-52. WHAT A YEAR!

Twenty headlines of events that occurred in 1998 are listed below. Other than having a number assigned to them, these headlines are in no order, so it is your job to organize them according to their proper category. Assign a group name and then, on a separate piece of paper write the numbers of the events that belong in that specific group. The number of groups is up to you. There is more than one way to organize these events.

1. Oprah Winfrey Wins Suit by Texas Cattle Ranchers

2. Nebraska and Michigan Share NCAA Football Title

3. President Suharto Reelected in Indonesia

4. Tobacco Companies Settle Lawsuit

5. Zhu Rongji Elected Premier in China

6. Yankees Win World Series in Four Games

7. Algerian Violence Contributes to Death Toll

8. University of Kentucky Captures NCAA Basketball Crown

9. Seinfeld Airs Final Episode

10. Telecommunications Merger Announced

11. Tornadoes Rip Through the South

12. General Motors Settles With Its Workers

13. Iraq Stops Weapons Inspections

14. Clinton Visits China

15. Central America Devastated by Hurricane Mitch

16. Legendary Singer Frank Sinatra Dies at 82

17. Titanic Wins 11 Academy Awards

18. Torrential Rains Cause Havoc in Northern California

19. Bulls Defeat Jazz for Another NBA Title

20. Estrada Elected Philippine President

4-53. WORKING WITH CLUSTERS

Writers use clusters to develop the subject they are writing about. They start with a nucleus word and then write down words that come to mind. They try to record each idea and then they circle each word after writing it down. Finally, they draw a line from that word to the closest related word. A sample cluster is shown below.

On a separate piece of paper, practice the cluster method using your own nucleus word. If you need suggestion words, try some of these: FITNESS; TRANSPORTATION; CELEBRITIES; YOUR TOWN OR CITY; DRIVER'S LICENSE.

Topic: **SELECTING A COLLEGE**

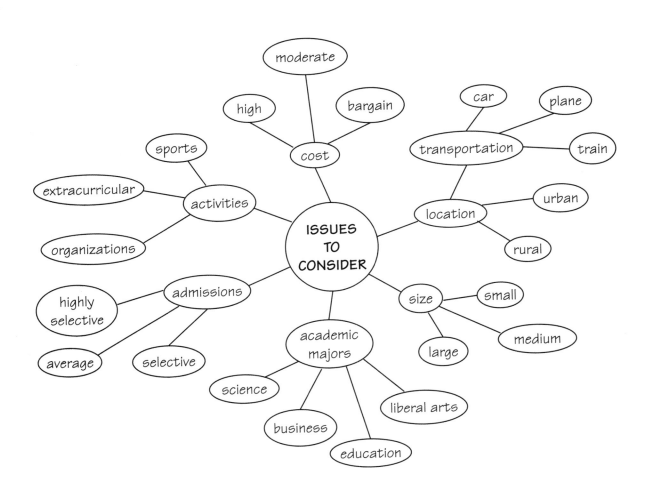

4-54. MORE WORK WITH CLUSTERS

When formulating and then arranging your thoughts, you might choose to use a method called clustering. Start with a nucleus word, a word related to your writing topic. Then write down other words that are associated with that nucleus word regardless of whether you think they are important at that time to your topic. Draw lines connecting these words. This cluster method will certainly help you to organize your ideas better. An example regarding English class homework is below.

On a separate piece of paper, develop your own cluster using a topic of your choice or one assigned by your teacher.

Topic: ENGLISH CLASS HOMEWORK ASSIGNMENTS

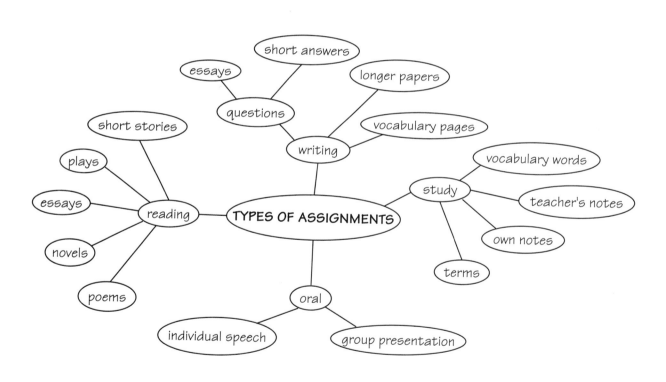

4-55. COMPOSING AN OUTLINE

Your outline is your guide, your game plan, your blueprint. Compose a thorough outline to make your writing more organized and convincing. Your working outline will probably go through several revisions before you begin to feel satisfied with it.

Using the outline format below, write your own outline on a topic of your choice. Remember that in your outline you are moving from the general to the specific. Each new division of your outline—as you move from the *Roman numeral* to the *capital letter* to the *Arabic numeral* to the *lower-case letter*—is more specific than the one preceding it. Include a thesis statement in your outline. Write your outline on a separate sheet of paper.

Topic: Moving away
Thesis statement: Moving away effects many changes.
Introduction
   I. Physical Changes *(topic)*
      A. New town *(subtopic)*
         1. Learning where necessary places are *(supporting detail)*
            a. School, doctor, dentist, church, stores *(specific example)*
      B. New house *(subtopic)*
         1. Getting used to all new rooms and property *(supporting detail)*
      C. New school *(subtopic)*
         1. Locating classrooms, cafeteria, gymnasium, auditorium *(supporting detail)*
         2. Knowing how to get from your new house to the school *(supporting detail)*
  II. Social Changes *(topic)*
      A. Meeting new friends *(subtopic)*
         1. Joining sports, clubs, and other activities *(supporting detail)*
         2. Confidence needed to begin socializing with new people *(supporting detail)*
      B. Maintaining former friendships from the former setting *(topic)*
         1. Methods *(supporting detail)*
            a. Phoning, writing letters, e-mail, visiting *(specific example)*
      C. Maintaining a balance of old and new friends *(subtopic)*
 III. Mental and Emotional Changes *(topic)*
      A. Problems *(subtopic)*
         1. Fitting in *(supporting detail)*
            a. Understanding the way the new people and places operate *(specific example)*
            b. Keeping one's individuality and yet blending in with the new *(specific example)*
         2. Missing the former setting *(supporting detail)*
            a. Remembering the memories of the "good old days" *(specific example)*
            b. Wondering what your friends are doing now *(specific example)*
      B. Good changes *(subtopic)*
         1. New opportunities *(supporting detail)*
            a. Fresh start with new friends, teachers, coaches *(specific example)*
            b. Maturity increases with these new challenges *(specific example)*
Conclusion

Name _____ Date _____ Period _____

4-56. MAKING SENSE WITH TOPIC OUTLINING

Efficient writers plan their writings. They think about the various aspects of their topic and how they will organize this material. Making an outline helps in this process. As a blueprint directs the construction crew, the outline serves as a guide for the writer. The success of the building depends on following the final blueprint. The success of the writing depends on following the final outline. Both the blueprint and the outline are painstakingly done. Neither is done only once. Reworking and revising are absolutely necessary.

Following the topic outline shown here, compose a similar outline for one of the topics listed. This topic outline is good for short essays such as those you write on examinations. Remember that in a topic outline, there are no specific details and no complete sentences. Include your own thesis statement in the outline. Write your outline on a separate sheet of paper.

TOPIC OUTLINE

Thesis statement: Summer is my favorite season.

Introduction
 I. Activities
    A. Swimming
    B. Picnics
    C. Water skiing
 II. Weather
    A. Warm
    B. Longer days and nights
    C. Light clothing
III. Leisure
    A. No school
    B. Sleep later in the morning
    C. Less responsibility
Conclusion

Choose from these topics:		
Parties	Aging	Writing
Exercise	Reading	College
Clothes	Work	Stress
Friends		

4-57. THE MIXED-UP OUTLINE

Mitch thought his outline was fairly well organized. His teacher, however, thought differently. Mitch was told to reorganize the subtopics, supporting details, and specific examples. On a separate sheet of paper, start from scratch and help Mitch compose a logical outline.

The topic is *A Teacher's Planning for the Academic Year.* Differentiate among the subtopics, supporting details, and specific details. Place the subtopics next to the Roman numerals, the supporting details next to the capital letters, and the specific examples next to the Arabic numbers. There are four subtopics, thirteen supporting details, and the rest are specific examples. The four subtopics (those with the asterisk) do not have to be in any specific order; neither do the supporting details for each subtopic. The same is true for the specific examples for the supporting details.

Topic: **A Teacher's Planning for the Academic Year**

Examinations
Observing students
Bathroom passes
* Developing the year's curriculum and activities
Goals and objectives
Change seat location
Time-out room
Homework assignment and collection
Excessive talking
Selecting and ordering materials
Developing lesson plans—units, weekly, daily
* Teaching methods
Lecture
Audio–visual
Lateness
Types of behavior problems
Inappropriate language
* Evaluating and assessing
Self-assessment
Student assessment
Discussion
Demonstration
Students teaching other students
* Classroom management
Developing classroom rules and procedures
Textbooks
Rubber bands, bulletin board posters
Throwing objects
Punishments for misbehaviors
Detention
Written assignment signed by parent or guardian

© 1999 by The Center for Applied Research in Education

4-58. STEPPING INTO ORGANIZATION

For any four of the following processes, list the steps (in chronological order) necessary to complete the process. Review the steps to make sure that the process works! Share your answers with your classmates. Write your answers on the lines provided. Once you know how to do this type of writing, you are on your way to writing clear instructions. Good luck!

1. Explain the mathematical operation showing that 1/2 divided by 1/4 equals 2. _____
   _____
   _____
   _____

2. Explain how to perform the operation of 12 times 13 equals 156. _____
   _____
   _____
   _____

3. Explain how eyeliner is applied. _____
   _____
   _____
   _____

4. Explain how to perform a corner kick in soccer. _____
   _____
   _____
   _____

5. Explain how to tie the laces of your running shoes. _____
   _____
   _____
   _____

6. Explain how to do a specific yo-yo trick. _____
   _____
   _____
   _____

4-59. PUTTING F. SCOTT FITZGERALD TOGETHER

Here are fifteen facts about American novelist and short-story writer F. Scott Fitzgerald. On a separate sheet of paper, group these facts, using their specific numbers, and then assign each group a name. Discuss your answers with your classmates.

1. born into a wealthy family in St. Paul, Minnesota in 1896

2. married Zelda Sayre in 1920

3. was a spokesman for the Jazz Age

4. created memorable characters including Jay Gatsby

5. was popularly known as Scott

6. his writings showed people who found their faiths in man shaken

7. named after Francis Scott Key, author of *"The Star-Spangled Banner"*

8. attended Princeton University, but did not receive a degree

9. served in the military

10. first novel was *This Side of Paradise* in 1920

11. Zelda and Scott lived in Europe and the United States

12. Zelda had an incurable mental illness and Fitzgerald had a breakdown

13. other novels include *The Great Gatsby, The Beautiful and the Damned,* and *Tender Is the Night*

14. died in 1940

15. was under emotional and financial pressures his last fifteen years

4-60. TELL ME A STORY

Since the dawn of time, people have told stories. These stories relate a sequence of events that interest the listener and teach the listener some thing(s) that he or she did not already know. A writer is a storyteller. Using the same methods as a storyteller, the writer entertains the reader. This method of storytelling is called narration.

Answer the following questions as you plan to write the narration. Then using that information, write the narration on a separate sheet of paper.

1. What event do you want to recall? _____

_____

_____

2. What is your purpose in telling this story? What do you want your reader to learn from this story? _____

_____

_____

3. Who is your audience? Is the story intended for a specific group? _____

_____

_____

4. How will you arrange the story? (a) straight chronological sequence; (b) final event first and then an explanation of the events leading up to that final event; (c) summarize the story first and then give the details of the events; (d) flashback

_____

5. What details will you include?_____

_____

_____

_____

_____

6. Will you use a first-person point of view (you are in the story) or a third-person point of view (you are not in the story)?

_____

7. What verb tense will you use? (a) present tense; (b) past tense. Regardless of the tense choice, be consistent in the verb tense. Do not shift tenses!

_____

_____

8. How will you show sentence variety in order to keep the reader's interest? _____

_____

_____

9. How will you capture the reader's interest from the start? _____

_____

_____

_____

_____

10. Here are a journalist's five traditional questions regarding narration. Answer these questions regarding your story.

(a) **Who** was involved in this event? _____

_____

_____

(b) **What** happened? _____

_____

_____

(c) **Where** did it happen? _____

_____

_____

(d) **Why** did it happen? _____

_____

_____

(e) **How** did it happen? _____

_____

_____

4-61. THE EVENT'S DETAILS

Using the journalist's traditional 5 W's and the 1 H to identify information, recreate the details of an event. It can be a sporting contest, a musical concert, an award ceremony, or some other event. On the lines provided, answer the questions regarding writing a narration. Your answers can be in the form of notes rather than complete sentences. Then, on another sheet of paper, write a rough draft of the event. Finally, using your teacher's suggestions, edit and improve the rough draft.

Name the event: _____

1. **Who** was involved? _____

   _____

2. **What** happened? (Give details.) _____

   _____

   _____

   _____

   _____

   _____

   _____

   _____

   _____

   _____

   _____

3. **Where** did it happen? _____

   _____

4. **When** did it happen? _____

   _____

5. **Why** did it happen? _____

   _____

   _____

   _____

   _____

4-61. THE EVENT'S DETAILS (cont'd)

6. **How** did it happen? _____

_____

_____

_____

7. How will you capture your reader's interest immediately? _____

_____

_____

8. In what order will you arrange the event's details? _____

_____

_____

9. What transition words or phrases will you use? _____

_____

_____

10. Will you use all five senses (sight, hearing, touch, taste, and smell) to recreate the event?
_____ If not, which ones will you use? _____

_____

11. What are you trying to emphasize in the retelling? _____

_____

_____

12. Will you use the first-person (I, we, me, our, mine, ours) or the third-person (he, she, it,
they) point of view? _____ Why?_____

_____

13. Do you want to include your attitude or impression about the event? _____ If so,
what is your attitude toward the event? _____

_____

14. Specifically, how will you get that attitude across to the reader?_____

_____

_____

15. If you choose to include dialogue, is it realistic and exact? _____

_____

© 1999 by The Center for Applied Research in Education

SKILLS

4-62. GETTING READY TO WRITE

Journalists use the five W's—Who? What? Where? When? Why? (as well as How?)—to identify the basics of their topic. So if a journalist had to cover a demonstration, for example, he or she would ask these questions to obtain the basic information about the demonstration. For each topic below, answer the 5 W's. Write your answers on the lines provided.

1. An incident that occurred in your school recently

Who? _____

What? _____

_____

Where? _____

_____

When? _____

_____

Why? (or How?) _____

_____

2. A scary experience

Who? _____

What? _____

_____

Where? _____

_____

When? _____

_____

Why? (or How?) _____

_____

3. An important event

Who? _____

4-62. GETTING READY TO WRITE (cont'd)

What? _____

_____

Where? _____

_____

When? _____

_____

Why? (or How?) _____

_____

4. A tragic event

Who? _____

What? _____

_____

Where? _____

_____

When? _____

_____

Why? (or How?) _____

_____

5. A funny incident

Who? _____

What? _____

_____

Where? _____

_____

When? _____

_____

Why? (or How?) _____

_____

4-63. OBSERVING BEFORE WRITING

Writers are very observant. Using their five senses, they are keen to what is happening around them. You will do the same in this activity. Select two experiences from the list below. Then fill in the required and appropriate information in note form. Use specific details. After that, select one experience and compose a paragraph in which you clearly relate what went on around you. Share your observations and writings with your classmates.

A sporting event	An interesting class	A humorous moment
A musical concert	A trip to a place	A tryout or an audition
A meal in the cafeteria	Some time at the mall	A test situation
A meal at home	A tense moment	A sad occasion

Experience _____

What did you hear? _____

_____

_____

What did you see? _____

_____

_____

What did you touch? _____

_____

_____

What did you smell? _____

_____

_____

What did you taste? _____

_____

_____

4-64. CHECKING OUT THE SENTENCES

Fifteen sentences that Kyle has written in his rough draft are below. Help out Kyle by correcting his mistakes. Each sentence has at least one error. Write the corrected version of the sentence on the appropriate line.

1. I ain't gonna go there now. _____

2. He is taller than her. _____

3. Me and him are going to the store real soon.

   _____

4. There is several ways to get their. _____

5. That cat of your's is quiet cute. _____

6. My sister new that you and me would go with her.

   _____

7. Theo likes bowling, skiing, and to go inline skating.

   _____

8. She will stay with them irregardless of the repercussions.

   _____

9. Will you please get off of the ledge? _____

10. There eager to find the way to get their. _____

11. Sum of the papers is hear now. _____

12. Monica learned me how to drive the auto mobile.

   _____

13. The winners, Ceil and him, are excepting the awards.

   _____

14. The record will be breaked tommorrow. _____

15. To who should I address this package? _____

4-65. BECOMING MORE SPECIFIC

The items in Column A are topics. The items in Column B are subtopics. The items in Column C are specific examples. Match the items in these three columns by writing the letters from columns B and C next to their appropriate match in Column A. Each of the 45 items is used only once.

Column A

1. _____ art
2. _____ automobiles
3. _____ colleges
4. _____ communication
5. _____ diseases
6. _____ education
7. _____ fitness
8. _____ furniture
9. _____ hygiene
10. _____ illegal actions
11. _____ junk food
12. _____ music
13. _____ radio
14. _____ reading materials
15. _____ vacations

Column B

A. aerobic activity
B. assault
C. baked goods
D. bed
E. California colleges
F. cancer
G. car care
H. exotic places
I. language
J. newspaper
K. painter
L. rock
M. skin care
N. stations
O. talk

Column C

AA. acid rock
BB. aggravated assault
CC. cakes
DD dialogue
EE. Grant Wood
FF. leukemia
GG. moisturizer
HH. oil change
II. queen
JJ. Spanish
KK. Stanford University
LL. stationary bike
MM. Tahiti
NN. *The New York Times*
OO. WALK-FM (97.5)

4-66. MOVING TOWARD PERFECTION

The classification essay writer moves from the general to the specific. Topics, subtopics, and specific categories are important components of the classification essay. Knowing how to become more specific is important in this type of writing.

   In the spaces below move from the *General Topic* to the *Specific* to the *More Specific* and finally to the *Most Specific*. Write your answers and then discuss your answers with your classmates. An example is done for you.

General Topic	Specific	More Specific	Most Specific
schools	colleges	private college	Hamilton College

1. animals _____ _____ _____

2. teachers _____ _____ _____

3. media _____ _____ _____

4. furniture _____ _____ _____

5. sports _____ _____ _____

6. buildings _____ _____ _____

7. entertainment _____ _____ _____

8. physical activity _____ _____ _____

9. summer events _____ _____ _____

10. workers _____ _____ _____

11. leaders _____ _____ _____

12. advertisements _____ _____ _____

13. relatives _____ _____ _____

14. types of writing _____ _____ _____

15. school tests _____ _____ _____

© 1999 by The Center for Applied Research in Education

4-67. "THE MORE EXACT VERBS" MAGIC SQUARE

Your verbs should be clear and exact because you want the reader to experience the action in the way you intend it to be experienced. Instead of saying "hearing," for example, why not use the word "eavesdropping" since it is exactly what the character is doing?

Match the general verb with its more specific mate. Write the general verb's number in the magic square's box containing its more specific mate. If your answers are correct, the rows, columns, and two diagonals will add up to the same number. Good luck!

A. underline	F. trounce	K. experiment	P. explain	U. lance
B. broadcast	G. quibble	L. agonize	Q. scan	V. batter
C. savor	H. abet	M. wander	R. hurl	W. caress
D. perturb	I. chatter	N. strut	S. clutch	X. comprehend
E. scrub	J. boost	O. transport	T. croon	Y. tumble

1. throw	6. try	11. talk	16. send	21. fall
2. bother	7. beat	12. sing	17. travel	22. defeat
3. bring	8. assist	13. mark	18. know	23. see
4. cut	9. hold	14. suffer	19. lift	24. taste
5. argue	10. wash	15. touch	20. tell	25. walk

A	B	C	D	E
F	G	H	I	J
K	L	M	N	O
P	Q	R	S	T
U	V	W	X	Y

89

4-68. THE DECLARATION OF INDEPENDENCE

As you research information for your writings, you will often come across difficult passages. Paraphrasing the sentence helps to better understand the sentence's essence. The language of the Declaration of Independence is not that easy. The signers of the Declaration had to understand what the text said before they could sign it.

Go back in time and take a close look at this document. On the lines following each excerpt, paraphrase the original quote. Use your dictionary if necessary. After all this, you will improve your paraphrasing techniques and know the Declaration of Independence better! (The text that follows is in its original form; hence, the capital letters showing up in expected places!)

1. ". . . that they (all Men) are endowed by their Creator with certain unalienable rights . . ."

   _____

2. "For imposing Taxes on us without our Consent:" _____

   _____

3. "He (King George III) has erected a Multitude of new Offices, and sent hither Swarms of Officers to harass our People . . . " _____

   _____

4. "He (King George III) has plundered our Seas, ravaged our Coasts, burnt our towns, and destroyed the Lives of our People." _____

   _____

5. "He (King George III) has constrained our fellow Citizens taken Captive on the high Seas to bear Arms against their Country, to be the Executioners of their Friends and Brethren."

   _____

6. "He (King George III) has refused his Assent to Laws, the most wholesome and necessary for the public good." _____

   _____

7. "He (King George III) has excited domestic Insurrections amongst us . . . " _____

   _____

8. "He (King George III) has affected to render the Military independent of, and superior to the Civil Power." _____

   _____

4-69. SAY IT WITHOUT SAYING IT

Good writers are clear and exact. They do not overstate the obvious, and they can tell you how to think without *directly* telling you how to think. When a writer states, "The senator scowled at his opponent," the reader understands the extent of the senator's anger because of the simple word **scowl.** Hence, the writer—without overstating—is clear, exact, and persuasive.

Directions: For each emotion or mood or characteristic below, write a sentence that illustrates that emotion. Use effective verbs, adjectives, and adverbs. Use a dictionary, if necessary.

1. joy: _____

_____

2. confusion: _____

_____

3. amazement: _____

_____

4. indifference: _____

_____

5. reflection: _____

_____

6. playfulness: _____

_____

7. hostility: _____

_____

8. concern: _____

_____

9. arrogance: _____

_____

10. friendliness: _____

_____

11. anxiety: _____

_____

12. eagerness: _____

_____

13. immaturity: _____

_____

14. pain: _____

_____

15. fright: _____

_____

4-70. DETAILS AND MOOD

Effective writings, particularly narratives and descriptions, include clear and concise details that help the reader understand the author's intention. Rather than the simple "house" image, the "battered sea shanty" is a more exact image.

    Improve each of the following vague images with a more precise image that connotes a mood or impression. After each new image, write the mood you wanted the reader to feel. Thus, the "battered sea shanty" evokes images of strength or age. Use a dictionary, if you wish.

  1. the country highway _____

  2. his football helmet _____

  3. the car _____

  4. Mrs. Santini's classroom _____

  5. the flag _____

  6. their radio _____

  7. the woman _____

  8. the tree _____

  9. our store _____

10. his hand _____

11. my grandmother's rug _____

12. my uncle's house _____

13. Mike's backpack _____

14. Li's sweater _____

15. a train _____

16. her hair _____

17. my bedroom _____

18. my sister's clock _____

19. Dad's uniform _____

20. Mom's pocketbook _____

4-71. ODD ONE OUT

Deciding what belongs and what does not belong in your composition takes some practice. This activity will serve as practice in eliminating that which does not belong with the other ideas or details. For each of these groups, draw a line through the word or term that does not belong with the other three. On the line following each group, write what the remaining three members have in common.

1. shed   shack   lean-to   mansion   _____

2. franc   peso   lira   nickel   _____

3. Jill   Nancy   Mary   John   _____

4. aluminum   gold   sugar   silver   _____

5. copperhead   cobra   eel   rattlesnake   _____

6. poodle   egret   Dalmatian   boxer   _____

7. Carter   Clinton   Roosevelt   Mondale   _____

8. Gemini   Puppy   Libra   Pisces   _____

9. Manitoba   Toronto   Alberta   Quebec   _____

10. kickball   soccer   basketball   football   _____

11. hat   enamel   skin   nose   _____

12. "Star Wars" "The Lion King" "Meet the Press" "Rocky"   _____

13. Peru   Brazil   Venezuela   Iceland   _____

14. orange   violet   indigo   black   _____

15. bicycle   train   plane   automobile   _____

16. morning   summer   winter   spring   _____

17. street   avenue   road   cloud   _____

18. Atlantic   Arctic   Indian   Mediterranean   _____

19. Sears Tower Fenway Park   World Trade Center Empire State Building _____

20. vanilla   strawberry   chocolate   blue   _____

4-72. ALL FOUR HAVE IT

Each group has four items. Find at least three things that the four group members share. Write their common traits on the lines provided.

Group One: gaga; lava; dodo; tutu

_____

_____

_____

Group Two: dither; rather; soothe; themes

_____

_____

_____

Group Three: Albany; Annapolis; Augusta; Austin

_____

_____

_____

Group Four: basketball; lacrosse; soccer; volleyball

_____

_____

_____

Group Five: bees; kite; soap; wood

_____

_____

_____

Group Six: hal; rod; tim; win

_____

_____

_____

Group Seven: kayak; skateboard; sled; surfboard

_____

_____

_____

4-73. WHAT DO THEY HAVE IN COMMON?

Writing a comparison–contrast piece requires an ability to see how two things are the same and how those same two things are different. William Shakespeare, for example, has Romeo compare Juliet to the sun. What immediate similarities do you see between these two? Start with the fact that both are bright, warm, and glowing, and you are on your way!

For each pair below, list two ways in which they are alike. Then list two ways in which they are different. Write your answers in note form on the appropriate lines. An example is done for you.

ice skates and snow sled

Alike: used for transportation; used for pleasure

Different: ice skates are tied to the body and the sled is not; ice skates have laces, but a sled

does not

1. **baseball bat and lacrosse stick**

Alike: _____

_____

Different: _____

_____

2. **human hand and human foot**

Alike: _____

_____

Different: _____

_____

3. **CD and vinyl record**

Alike: _____

_____

Different: _____

_____

4. **horse and dog**

Alike: _____

_____

Different: _____

_____

5. **Michael Jordan and Anna Kournikova**

Alike: _____

_____

Different: _____

_____

6. **one of your relatives and another of your relatives**

Alike: _____

_____

Different: _____

_____

7. **English class and math class**

Alike: _____

_____

Different: _____

_____

8. **two television programs** _____ and _____

Alike: _____

_____

Different: _____

_____

9. **two movies** _____ and _____

Alike: _____

_____

Different: _____

_____

10. **two board games** _____ and _____

Alike: _____

_____

Different: _____

_____

Name _____ Date _____ Period _____

4-74. WRITING HEADLINES AND SUMMARIES

A necessary writer's skill is creating convincing and concise headlines and summaries. Here you will do the same with different forms of entertainment, including watching television!

Select two different forms of entertainment. Movies, television programs, and books are some choices. For each area, creatively capture the main idea for the headline. Then compose a one-line summary sentence that sums up the main idea of the work. Finally, write a longer summary of the work. Share your answers with your classmates. An example is given to you.

Work: *Romeo and Juliet*

Headline: Feuding Families' Kids Found Dead

One-line summary: Romeo Montague and Juliet Capulet, children of the feuding families, kill themselves.

Longer summary: The Montagues and Capulets of Verona, Italy, have been feuding for years. At a Capulet party, Romeo Montague, 16, meets and falls in love with Juliet Capulet, 14. The whirlwind romance of these star-crossed lovers leads to their secret marriage by Friar Laurence. Romeo, having killed Juliet's cousin Tybalt in a brawl, is banished from Verona and is staying in Mantua. Unaware that Juliet is now Romeo's wife, Juliet's parents want her to marry Count Paris. Friar Laurence's potion plan for Juliet backfires when Romeo, seeing Juliet in her family's mausoleum, mistakenly thinks her dead and drinks his purchased poison. Awaking immediately after Romeo has taken the poison, Juliet stabs herself. Seeing their children dead, the feuding families end their dispute and erect statues to honor the memories of Romeo and Juliet.

Work: _____

Headline: _____

One-line summary: _____

_____

Longer summary: _____

_____

_____

_____

_____

_____

_____

_____

_____

_____

_____

_____

_____

_____

_____

Work: _____

Headline: _____

One-line summary: _____

_____

Longer summary: _____

_____

_____

_____

_____

_____

_____

_____

_____

_____

4-75. HOW TO PRESENT IT

Your teacher has assigned these topics. You are permitted to present each topic in any way you choose. On the lines provided, list two ways in which you could present the topic. For each method of presentation, briefly tell how you would go about developing the topic. Suggestions include description, narration, example, analysis, classification, process analysis, comparison and contrast, definition, and cause and effect. An example is done for you.

My school's gymnasium

(a) *description:* I would describe the physical appearance of the gym starting with the ceiling and walls and moving on to the bleachers, floor, and equipment. Then I would describe the gym on the night of an exciting athletic event.

(b) *narration:* I would tell a story of a worker who helped to build the gym many years ago. I would have him thinking about his creation and the memories this gym will bring to many students and their families. I would have him, as he is placing bricks or nailing the floorboards, dream of the happy and sad times ahead for the people who will sit and play in this gym.

1. **The shopping mall**

(a) _____

_____

_____

(b) _____

_____

_____

2. **Friendship**

(a) _____

_____

_____

(b) _____

_____

_____

3. **Your Town—Today and Yesterday**

(a) _____

4-75. HOW TO PRESENT IT (cont'd)

_____

_____

(b) _____

_____

_____

4. Pets

(a) _____

_____

_____

(b) _____

_____

_____

5. Movies' popularity

(a) _____

_____

_____

(b) _____

_____

_____

6. The Internet

(a) _____

_____

_____

(b) _____

_____

_____

7. Dreams

(a) _____

_____

_____

(b) _____

_____

_____

TYPES OF WRITINGS

4-76. START WITH THIS

Complete each of these 15 open-ended sentences. Then, on a separate sheet of paper, use that sentence as the opening sentence in a story or essay. Check for proper grammar, mechanics, and usage. Make the writing as interesting as possible. Share your final product with your classmates.

1. The future is _____

2. If only _____

3. My favorite vacation place is _____

4. A good summer job is _____

5. Things would be very different if _____

   _____

6. Exercise can be _____

7. Ten years from now I _____

8. My favorite movie is _____

9. We never thought that _____

   _____

10. It was not as _____

    as I thought it would be when _____

11. Peer pressure is _____

12. My school should _____

13. Sometimes adults are _____

14. One school rule that should be changed is _____

    _____

15. One of the world's most powerful people is _____

    _____

4-77. HERE IS YOUR LIFE

Recalling events in your life is a good way to select and then develop ideas for your writings. On the lines below, list some important events in your life. List the event's approximate date. Then briefly tell why each event was significant. Why was it important to you? Start with your birth and move on to the other events in your life, trying to list them in sequential order (as well as possible). Use this list as an inventory of possible writing topics.

Date	*Event*	*Significance*
_____	_____	_____
_____	_____	_____
_____	_____	_____
_____	_____	_____
_____	_____	_____
_____	_____	_____
_____	_____	_____
_____	_____	_____
_____	_____	_____

4-78. TODAY'S JOURNAL

Use this sheet to record interesting things that you see, hear, or do today. Simply write what you see, hear, or do and your immediate ideas and reactions to it. There is no need to write these down in any formal way using sentences and proper grammar. Rather than simply experiencing a moment and then possibly forgetting about it, you can then use these recordings and reflections as a writing topic in the near future. Enjoy and stay alert!

_____

_____

_____

_____

_____

_____

_____

_____

_____

_____

_____

_____

_____

_____

_____

_____

_____

_____

_____

_____

_____

_____

4-79. FREE WRITING

Take the next ten minutes and write about whatever you want to. Let your ideas go wherever they take you. There is no assigned direction or designated goal—explore and see where you land. Then, after you have completed the writing, exchange your writing with a partner. He or she will read your free writing and, on a separate sheet of paper, list possible topics that were found in your free writing. You will do the same to his or her writing. In this way you have both opened up new writing possibilities and directions!

_____

_____

_____

_____

_____

_____

_____

_____

_____

_____

_____

_____

_____

_____

_____

_____

_____

_____

_____

4-80. JOURNAL WRITING

One way to gather ideas for possible writings is to keep a writer's journal in which you record your feelings, thoughts, and the events of that particular day. Read the following sample journal entry. Then, on the lines provided, list some possible topics included in the entry that this student could write about.

Today Grandfather remarried. He had met Flo ten years ago. That was about three years after Grandma passed away. The wedding was not very elaborate. It was held at the local VFW and about 30 people attended. Music was provided by Young at Heart, a group of musicians, all senior citizens. Everybody there had a good time. I often think about when I will be old like Grandpa. Will I still have my health? Will I have enough money to live comfortably? Will I have kids? Grandchildren? Where will I be living then?

The science project is not going along as well as I hoped. My lab partner and I are not very organized. Even if we were, it is hard to meet during the day since we don't have the same free periods. After school both of us are very busy with sports and other extracurricular activities. Mr. Pearson said that for each day the project is late, there will be a ten-point deduction from the project's final grade.

Why do all the television stations have to emphasize the bad news? There is very little to cheer about while watching the nightly news? Are people tired of seeing only bad stuff or am I alone in feeling this way? Murders, robberies, floods, fires, and the rest can depress me.

My history teacher's wife has just passed her medical school exams and is going to be a doctor. They have three children who are now grown. Mrs. Friedland decided she wants to become a pediatrician. I guess she misses kids and will get to see enough of them as a pediatrician. I hope she likes being a doctor.

Possible topics include:

_____   _____

_____   _____

_____   _____

_____   _____

_____   _____

_____   _____

_____   _____

4-81. BEING THERE

An important type of writing is the descriptive paragraph. A writer must make the reader feel he or she is there taking in the scene. Use your five senses to describe each location. If you have not been physically present at such a location, imagine that you are there. The answers can be factual or fictional, but they should be reasonable. They should be notes instead of complete sentences. Write your answers on the appropriate lines. Use the back of the sheet for extra space.

1. **A relative's house**

see: _____

hear: _____

touch: _____

taste: _____

smell: _____

2. **A classroom just before a very challenging test is to start**

see: _____

hear: _____

touch: _____

taste: _____

smell: _____

3. **A train station during rush hour**

see: _____

hear: _____

touch: _____

© 1999 by The Center for Applied Research in Education

taste: _____

smell: _____

4. A movie theater in the middle of a scary movie segment

see: _____

hear: _____

touch: _____

taste: _____

smell: _____

5. A hospital's emergency room

see: _____

hear: _____

touch: _____

taste: _____

smell: _____

6. A nursery school birthday party

see: _____

hear: _____

touch: _____

taste: _____

smell: _____

4-82. ORGANIZING SOME WRITING SITUATIONS

Your teacher has given you the following writing assignments. List at least four subtopics that you will include. An example is done for you. Share your ideas with your classmates.

Topic	Subtopics
Your House or Apartment:	architecture, location, size, cost, room arrangements, decorations, age

1. A friend: _____
   _____

2. Your school: _____
   _____

3. A specific movie: _____
   _____

4. Planning a vacation: _____
   _____

5. A specific automobile: _____
   _____

6. Methods of transportation: _____
   _____

7. Types of music: _____
   _____

8. Types of jobs: _____
   _____

9. Communication: _____
   _____

10. Bodies of water: _____
    _____

4-83. KNOWING YOUR AUDIENCE

An important concern you have as a writer is knowing your reader/audience. Who will be reading your composition, letter, or report? Is your reader a newspaper editor, a fourth-grader, or a senator? Obviously, your vocabulary, sentence structure, and depth of thoughts will depend on who is reading your writing. How you communicate to this reader is of paramount importance.

Select two of the following situations. For each, write a paragraph keeping your audience in mind. Write your responses on a separate sheet of paper. Be prepared to explain why you selected the vocabulary, details, sentence structure, and other devices.

1. Write a letter to your school's principal expressing your dissatisfaction with the plan to increase the school day by ninety minutes. *(Write only the body of the letter.)*

2. Write a letter to a fifth-grader asking him/her to participate in the JUMP FOR LIFE jump-rope contest to be held at his/her school on the twentieth of next month. Explain about getting pledges to support his/her efforts and that the money collected will be used by the American Heart Association for heart disease research. *(Write only the body of the letter.)*

3. Write a letter to your local political representative letting him/her know that you oppose the plan to place factories where the existing Little League fields are. *(Write only the body of the letter.)*

4. Write a letter to the editor of your local newspaper expressing your concern that high school sports are not given enough space in the newspaper. *(Write only the body of the letter.)*

5. Write an article for your school newspaper giving reasons why so few students participate in extracurricular activities.

6. Recently your town's board has voted that only those students with a B+ average or higher can work for the town during the summer months. Write a letter to the town board expressing your opinion on this recent legislation. *(Write only the body of the letter.)*

7. Explain to an eight-year-old how it is better to walk away from a possible fight than to become involved in it.

8. Write a letter to the CD company that has incorrectly billed you for an additional thirty-five dollars. *(Write only the body of the letter.)*

4-84. HERE'S A START

Sometimes coming up with a story's first line is the toughest part of the writing assignment. To make the situation less troublesome, this list of 15 story starters has been furnished for you. Use any of these sentences as the first line of your story. Use another sheet of paper for the story.

1. The elderly couple looked at each other.

2. Never before had Juan found himself in such a frightening situation.

3. Lara had not studied for this major examination and now the teacher was handing out the question sheet.

4. Jerry had not seen the car make the turn.

5. She slowly dialed his number and hoped he would be there to answer the telephone.

6. Three police officers approached the car.

7. Paula had anticipated what her mother would say about it.

8. He was the kind of man who would always be there to help, but this time . . .

9. When the doorbell rang, five-year-old Kaneesha raced to open the door.

10. The rocket's liftoff seemed ill-fated from the start.

11. Rosa had promised herself she would not let this happen.

12. The tabloids had first related the facts surrounding the case.

13. With her husband and children waiting outside the doctor's office, Mrs. Blandino listened as the doctor told her the news.

14. A class reunion can be an interesting experience.

15. As the lead runners neared the 25-mile marker, the marathon became very exciting.

© 1999 by The Center for Applied Research in Education

4-85. WHICH WRITING METHOD?

Writers can approach a subject in several interesting ways. The following five methods and associated questions help writers consider a subject. Examples are given for each method's explanation. Use the methods below for any one of the eight subjects. Write your answers (in note form) on the lines provided. Discuss your answers with your classmates.

Methods:

Sensory Description: Using your five senses, describe the subject. (a carnival; an apple; a VCR)

Comparison: Compare it to something/someone else showing its similarities and its differences. (two poems; two methods of fishing; two horses)

Analysis and Classification: Classify and analyze its components. (U.S. and British governments; two teachers' grading systems; two bowlers' techniques)

Application: What is its function? (camcorder; exercise bike; hair dryer)

Opinion: Assess its worth. (athlete's abilities and contributions to his/her team; benefits of swimming; mutual funds or individual stocks)

Possible subjects:

(a) an apple; (b) a summer's day at the beach; (c) a difficult school examination; (d) an athletic team practice; (e) your family's car; (f) diets; (g) the perfect birthday party; (h) a funeral

Subject: _____

Sensory Description: _____

_____

Comparison: _____

_____

Analysis and Classification: _____

_____

Application: _____

_____

Opinion: _____

_____

4-86. IDEAS FOR COMPARING AND CONTRASTING

For each pair, write one possible comparison (how they are alike) or contrast (how they are different). Then, on the back of this sheet, write two points of comparison or contrast for each pair. An example is done for you for each heading.

COMPARISONS

New York City and Los Angeles: A. Both are large cities. B. Both have respected universities. C. Both are heavily populated.

1. **Baseball and Softball:** _____

2. **Television and Radio:** _____

3. **Bicycles and Subways:** _____

4. **Canada and England:** _____

5. **Triangles and Circles:** _____

CONTRASTS

***The New York Times* and *Time* magazine:** A. One is a daily and one is a weekly publication. B. Their paper textures are not the same. C. One has several separate sections (Metro, Sports, and more); the other cannot be separated.

6. **Wheelbarrels and Dump trucks:** _____

7. **Dime and Quarter:** _____

8. **Cell phones and Wall phones:** _____

9. **Two different vacation locations:** _____

10. **Two different friends:** _____

Name _____ Date _____ Period _____

4-87. SENSORY DESCRIPTIONS

A writer often describes a place or an event using the five senses. What the writer sees, hears, touches, tastes, and smells are important in conveying the experience. Following the example below, use the five-senses approach to describe a place or an experience. Choose your own topic or the topic(s) assigned by your teacher. Since your notes are part of the rough draft for a later writing, they do not have to be in complete sentences. Write the answers on the lines provided.

Experience: A DAY AT THE AMUSEMENT PARK

see: other customers, vendors, rides, security guards, ride operators, buildings, arcades, sky, vending machines

hear: music, announcements, people talking, machines, rides

touch: food, rides, money, another's hands

taste: cotton candy, hot dogs, soda, hamburgers, popcorn

smell: food, rides' exhaust, sea breezes

Possible topics include Graduation Day, your birthday party, a day at the beach, a wedding, a funeral, an athletic contest, or a day at your school.

Experience or Place: _____

see: _____

hear: _____

touch: _____

taste: _____

smell: _____

Experience or Place: _____

see: _____

hear: _____

touch: _____

taste: _____

smell: _____

4-88. PLEASE EXPLAIN HOW TO DO IT

Explaining how to change a bicycle's tire, how to program a computer, or how to cook a specific meal share at least one common trait. Each explains the chronological sequence of stages and steps necessary to attain a specific goal. This very useful and informative type of writing is called an *instructions explanation*.

Your goal is to write a clear stage-by-stage—including steps within the stages—instructions explanation composition for one of the eight tasks below. First, select one of the tasks. Then write a rough draft of how to accomplish that task. Then, on the spaces provided, answer the following questions to help check on and improve your writing. Finally, on a separate sheet of paper, write the good copy of the instructions explanation composition for your chosen task.

Select one of these tasks: (a) how to make a peanut butter and jelly sandwich; (b) how to shoot a foul shot; (c) how to tune a guitar; (d) how to get from your house to school; (e) how to tie a shoe; (f) how to make a three-point turn; (g) how to lose weight sensibly; (h) how to play "Mary Had a Little Lamb" on the piano

1. Quite simply, who is your audience? _____

2. Are your stages for this process in strict sequential order? _____

3. Are your stages broken up into steps that are in strict sequential order? _____

4. Have you included *all* the stages and steps? _____

5. Have you mentally or physically run through the process to ensure that it will work? _____

6. Are the stages and steps detailed enough for the reader to understand what he or she must do? _____

7. Have you included transitions such as *first, then, while, finally,* and other similar words and phrases? _____

8. Have you defined the terms that might be unfamiliar to the reader? _____

9. Have you clearly indicated the place, for example, *near the corner* or *by the lamp,* to help your reader follow the directions more easily? _____

10. Have you specified the reasons for each stage and step? _____

11. Have you used the present tense for your verbs? _____

© 1999 by The Center for Applied Research in Education

4-89. THE PERSUASIVE ESSAY

The purpose behind a persuasive essay is to persuade the reader to change his or her opinion. Both style and substance contribute to the persuasive essay's power and success. Using logical thinking and cogent, supporting evidence, the writer strives to validate his or her opinion and persuade the reader to agree with or at least recognize the author's stance on this issue.

Select one of the thesis statements below. Read the questions writers consider before writing a persuasive essay. Then, on a separate sheet of paper, write your persuasive essay defending (or arguing against) the thesis statement. Finally, review the questions before composing the good copy of your persuasive essay.

Thesis Statements

- There should be no smoking in restaurants.
- Laboratory testing involving animals should be eliminated.
- The school year should be increased by an additional twenty days.
- Capital punishment is a deterrent to crime.
- Minors should be allowed to buy cigarettes.
- Book banning in public schools is a violation of the First Amendment.
- During their four years of high school, students should perform a minimum of 50 hours of community service as part of their graduation requirement.
- Euthanasia should be allowed for those wishing to end their lives.
- The benefits of coeducational gym classes outweigh the drawbacks.
- Working more than 15 hours each week is detrimental to students' academic success.

1. Is the issue both important (to the reader) and arguable?

2. Who is your audience?

3. Have you stated the thesis statement near the essay's beginning?

4. Is your argument reasonable and logical?

5. Are you appealing to the reader's ethical, emotional, and/or rational sensibilities?

6. Is your essay clearly and logically organized?

7. Are solid, convincing supporting details in the form of facts and/or examples and/or experts' opinions included?

8. Did you use the first- or third-person point of view? Why?

9. Did you consider the opposing viewpoint in your essay?

10. Did you reword or restate the thesis statement near the essay's conclusion?

If you have done most of these well, you have probably proven your thesis statement.

4-90. WHAT IF?

Writers and inventors are alike in that they share the idea of "What if...?" What if the Martians landed? What if the world's food supply became scarce? What if the automobile became outmoded? These are some questions that great minds think about whether fiction or fact.

Here you are asked to do the same. Ten hypothetical situations are posed. Write a few possible changes you would see if the situation actually came true. Your responses should be notes, not complete sentences. An example is done for you.

What if the typical school week were three days instead of five?
more homework; longer school days; find more hobbies to pass the time; greater dependence upon oneself to learn; more responsibilities at home

1. What if you were born as a member of the opposite sex?

_____

_____

_____

2. What if you moved two thousand miles away next month?

_____

_____

_____

3. What if summer were twice as long as it is now?

_____

_____

_____

4. What if you were twice as intelligent as you are now?

_____

_____

_____

5. What if the highway speed limit were doubled?

_____

_____

_____

6. What if you were a teen during the time your grandparents were teens?

_____

_____

_____

7. What if the world's population doubled in the next hundred years?

_____

_____

_____

8. What if the world's population halved during the next hundred years?

_____

_____

_____

9. What if airplane travel was disallowed for the next ten years?

_____

_____

_____

10. What if doctors found a way to attach a third arm to the human body?

_____

_____

_____

ANSWER KEYS

4-1. LOOKING WITHIN (AND WITHOUT)

Answers will vary.

4-2. SEARCHING FOR THE TOPIC

Answers will vary.

4-3. WRITING JOGGERS

Answers will vary.

4-4. THE TWO-MINUTE DRILL

Answers will vary.

4-5. LISTING

Answers will vary.

4-6. WE THINK ALIKE (AND DIFFERENTLY)

Answers will vary.

4-7. BRAINSTORMING WORD-FIND

```
K F R G Y W H A L T D C W M B R E X T K N C O Q
B A P E C T L T C L P O B N T M W C G T Z Q P W
W B R A V E R Y K T H A L L O W E E N U R S E S
L G R S G A M E J I I S Q P R I Y J I E N K R M
Y S T T V E T O B Q T N P X H T T V F C L T A H
F P Y E Q J A B V I W T G Q I W A R V S O J R
K R L R U A G N P I L Z E N R B N L U Z T K I K
N B J P I N M O T X N T U N S R Z S S D N G Z V
T V W T Z U B I N S S G S N S J S Z T G A B X D
Z Y J B Z A V T D W Y G F Z T J X Z M V R R Q Q
Z O O S E R N A W C O C K L Q N K D X K U X G B
S P G C S Y G R F R G V K J B K Z S X L A K R Q
Q G W G V R R G F C U N K Q B T N Q C T T C W P
K N L C D L C I L K R X M C P L J W P C S F L J
P Z P C X V Q M Q Y T S L H G B M R R K E D N D
T T W F C D V M C N Z Z Q N H L R D N G R K D N
M T G K G G C I T C N Z X L B F R P X F R L D Q
```

4-8. TAKE FOUR

Answers will vary.

4-9. BRAINSTORMING INTO A COMPOSITION

Answers will vary.

4-10. BRAINSTORMING . . . THE START OF THE WRITING PROCESS

Answers will vary.

4-11. MAKING LISTS

Possible answers include the following. They are not listed in any specific order of importance.

War: cause, purpose, risks, reasons for involvement, participants, armaments, recruitment, news reporting, loss of lives, financial costs, leadership, strategy

Newspapers: purpose, sources, audience, financial costs, writers, features, philosophy, advertisers, delivery, sales force, sales location

Selecting a college: admissions criteria, degree requirements, cost, academic offerings, class size, living and dining facilities, campus setting, location, social life

4-12. COOPERATIVE LISTING OF IDEAS

Answers will vary.

4-13. EAVESDROPPING AT THE MALL

Answers will vary.

4-14. SETTING THE TERMS

4-15. GETTING THE TERMS DOWN

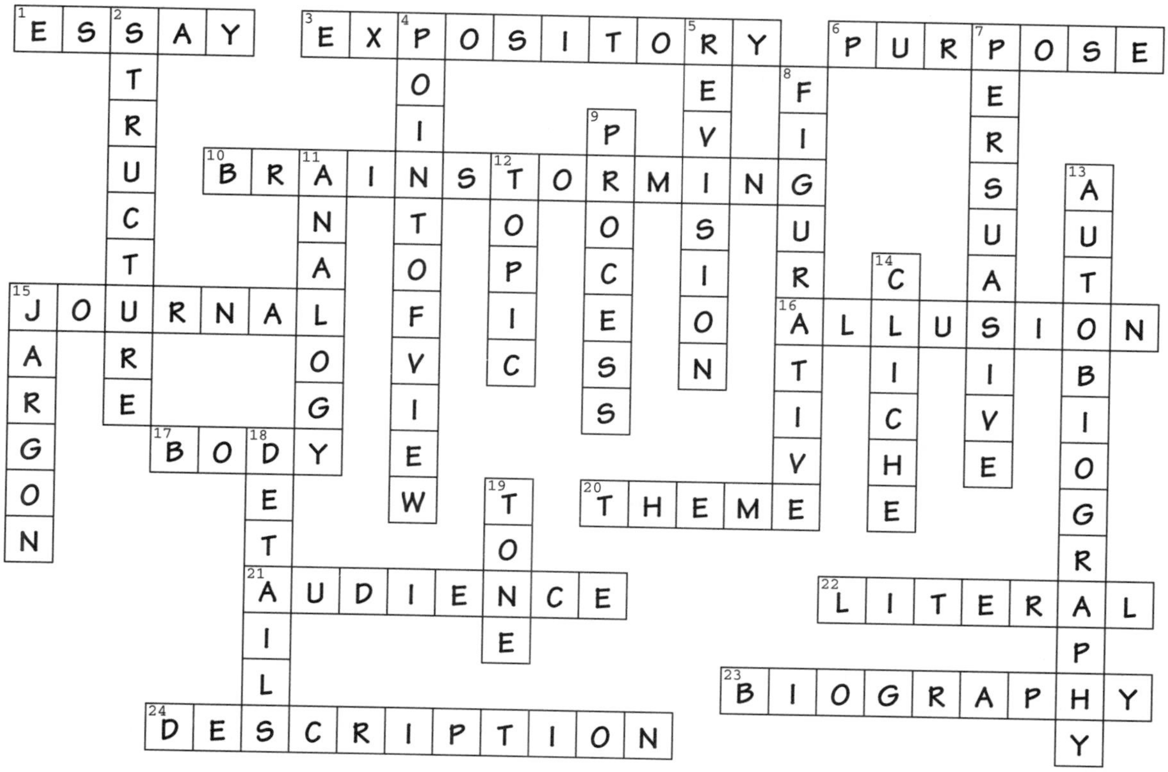

Crossword grid (filled answers):

- 1 Across: ESSAY
- 3 Across: EXPOSITORY
- 6 Across: PURPOSE
- 10 Across: BRAINSTORMING
- 15 Across: JOURNAL
- 16 Across: ALLUSION
- 17 Across: BODY
- 20 Across: THEME
- 21 Across: AUDIENCE
- 22 Across: LITERAL
- 23 Across: BIOGRAPHY
- 24 Across: DESCRIPTION

- 2 Down: STRUCTURE
- 4 Down: POINTOFVIEW
- 5 Down: PERSUASIVE
- 7 Down: PERSUASIVE
- 8 Down: FIGURATIVE
- 9 Down: PROCESS
- 11 Down: ANALOGY
- 12 Down: TOPIC
- 13 Down: AUTOBIOGRAPHY
- 14 Down: CLICHE
- 15 Down: JARGON
- 18 Down: DETAIL
- 19 Down: TONE

4-16. TALK IT OUT

Answers will vary.

4-17. RESEARCH TOOLS

A = 13	B = 3	C = 6	D = 12
E = 8	F = 10	G = 15	H = 1
I = 11	J = 5	K = 4	L = 14
M = 2	N = 16	O = 9	P = 7

Each row, column, and diagonal adds up to 34.

4-18. RESEARCH MATCHING COLUMN

1. J	5. O	9. C	13. A
2. I	6. G	10. K	14. N
3. M	7. D	11. P	15. B
4. F	8. E	12. L	16. H

The man's name is JIM (1–3). The weather condition is FOG (4–6). The ship's part is the DECK (7–10). The synonym for strategy is PLAN (11–14). The twenty-third U.S. president's initials are BH [Benjamin Harrison] (15–16).

4-19. IN THE LIBRARY

1. A call number is used to locate the book in the library.
2. 10
3. (b) 330
4. (b) 370
5. author, subject, and title
6. author's last name
7. movie directors
8. S. Pond
9. Prem (Premiere)
10. 3
11. the volume number of the magazine
12. October
13. 1996
14. "One Man's Band"
15. illustrated

4-20. WHICH MAGAZINE?

1. RE	6. ES	11. LL	16. AR
2. AD	7. TS	12. US	17. CH
3. ER	8. PO	13. TR	18. AEO
4. SD	9. RT	14. AT	19. LO
5. IG	10. SI	15. ED	20. GY

The three magazines are *Reader's Digest*, *Sports Illustrated*, and *Archaeology*.

4-21. MATCHING THE TITLE AND THE FIRST LINE

1. H	3. B	5. G	7. F
2. C	4. D	6. E	8. A

Reasons

Students' wording will vary, but these are the points to be made.

1. Changing slowly or gracefully . . .
2. Each wave of water (or business) is significant.
3. When a voice is *dubbed*, it is *doubled*.
4. A face can be made up for $10.
5. When the outside conditions are nasty, it is said we brave the elements.
6. Teeth bite.
7. Cocaine is white; the "line" of justice; lawyers supposedly uphold justice.
8. Teens are quitting smoking.

4-22. WHICH SOURCE?

1. B, C, E
2. B, C, E
3. A
4. B, D, E
5. E
6. B, D, E
7. B, D, E
8. A
9. A, B, C, E
10. B, D, E
11. B, C, E
12. B, E
13. B, C, E
14. B, D, E
15. A, B, D, E

4-23. YOU CAN FIND IT

Here are the answers. Students will find the information in various sources.

1. A ciseaux is a jump in which both legs open while in the air.
2. approximately four hours
3. Sagittarius
4. Miami Dolphins
5. A Druze is a member of a religious sect in Syria and Lebanon.
6. Kampala is the capital of Uganda.
7. Toronto, Ontario
8. A *campesino* is a peasant or a farmer.
9. the parachute
10. Benvenuto Cellini
11. George Orwell
12. protagonist
13. Robert Pinsky
14. 1975
15. 1973

4-24. LOCATING INFORMATION

These are possible sources; there can be additional sources.

1. conversations with relatives; photograph albums; family letters
2. encyclopedia; Internet; history books; interview with soldiers and/or veterans; television programs; filmstrips
3. Internet; encyclopedia; science books; interview with scientists; weather books
4. Manhattan College personnel; Internet; college profile books; interview past and present Manhattan College students
5. Internet; encyclopedia; biography; autobiography; history books; almanac
6. Internet; encyclopedia; information from the foundation itself; science books
7. Internet; history books; encyclopedia; art books
8. Internet; *Newsday* personnel; book on cartoonist
9. Internet; encyclopedia; mythology books; art books
10. encyclopedia; Internet; music book; biography; autobiography; music critics' writings
11. history book; Internet; science book; encyclopedia; San Francisco Historical Society
12. Internet; encyclopedia; education reference sources; Australian education pamphlets
13. Internet; encyclopedia; history books; books about newspapers
14. history books; Internet; Attica Prison personnel and historical notes
15. science books; Internet; health books; encyclopedia

4-25. WHERE CAN YOU FIND IT?

Here are the correct answers. Students will find the information in various sources.

1. foot	6. 1963	11. Atomic Mass Unit
2. Neil A. Armstrong	7. Eric the Red	12. Lisbon
3. Bisons	8. Salmon P. Chase	13. Ophelia
4. Clara Barton	9. Mt. Sunflower	14. Cooperstown
5. Henry Cavendish	10. Raymond Chandler	15. *Softly*

4-26. LET'S GO AND FIND IT

1. a county in Wales
2. a Jewish theater group
3. a Roman emperor from A.D. 117–138
4. a book or writing about the lives of the saints
5. Ethiopia's emperor from 1930–1936 and 1941–1974
6. an American football player and coach
7. an English astronomer

8. an American actor, race car driver, and food maker
9. the patron saint of youth
10. an insoluble problem
11. an American painter
12. a former American Olympic track and field hero
13. a British poet
14. in New York City
15. *Keepers*
16. a shrub
17. a film
18. the drachma
19. Ontario
20. Scotland

4-27. FINDING THE ANSWERS

Here are the answers. The sources will vary.

1. (a) John
2. Butch Cassidy and the Sundance Kid
3. six
4. Judaism
5. Leslie Lynch King, Jr.
6. William Henry Harrison
7. *A Tale of Two Cities*
8. 116 years
9. D-Day
10. New York City
11. Cream
12. badminton
13. the ear
14. Alberta
15. (d) khaki

4-28. "RESEARCHING THE ANSWERS" CONTEST

1. Self-contained underwater breathing apparatus
2. Ben Shahn
3. a boat
4. Henryk Sienkiewicz
5. Canada
6. Treaty of Ghent

7. Patty Sheehan
8. Graduate Record Examination(s)
9. 1857
10. Stone (Lucy Stone and Irving Stone)
11. *Scarlett* by Alexandra Ripley
12. England
13. British Columbia
14. Judas Iscariot
15. Ella Fitzgerald
16. *Our American Cousin*
17. Frederick III, Elector of Saxony
18. Freya
19. baseball
20. Massapequa

4-29. DICTIONARY MAGIC SQUARE

A = 15	B = 6	C = 9	D = 4
E = 12	F = 1	G = 14	H = 7
I = 2	J = 11	K = 8	L = 13
M = 5	N = 16	O = 3	P = 10

Each row, column, and diagnoal adds up to 34.

4-30. THE 5 W'S AND THE 1 H

Answers will vary.

4-31. YOUR NOTE CARDS

Answers will vary.

4-32. TAKING INVENTORY

Answers will vary.

4-33. SOME IDEAS FOR YOU

No answers necessary.

4-34. TAKING A CLOSER LOOK AT YOURSELF

Answers will vary.

4-35. FINDING THE TOPICS FROM A TO Z

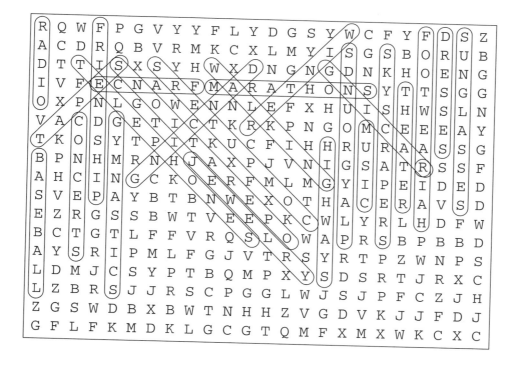

4-36. TWENTY-FIVE HIDDEN TOPICS

4-37. TAKE FIVE MINUTES

Answers will vary.

4-38. LETTING YOUR MIND WANDER

Answers will vary.

4-39. QUESTIONS

Answers will vary.

4-40. TOPIC, SUB-TOPICS, AND FACTS

These are possible subtopics and their facts (numbers).

Land: 5, 10, 11, 20
People: 1, 8, 12, 16
History: 2, 9, 14, 17
Economy: 3, 7, 13, 19
Government: 4, 6, 15, 18

4-41. SUPPORTING THE TOPIC

Answers will vary.

4-42. WHAT TO INCLUDE

These are sample answers.

1. Literature . . . types of literature, examples of the types of literature, characteristics of good literature, noted authors
2. The school dropout . . . characteristics of the dropout, causes of dropping out, effects of dropping out
3. The Turmoil of the 1960s . . . political happenings, riots, media contributions, protesters
4. How to study for an exam . . . physical setting, study methods, concentration level, intelligence
5. The road to better physical health . . . eating habits, exercise, reading about the subject
6. Getting published . . . idea for published work, query letter, submitting proposal, sample chapter

7. Taking better photographs . . . setting, equipment, personal characteristics of photographers

8. Selecting the right college . . . talking with your guidance counselor, reading college catalogues, visiting the school, talking to college's students

9. Friendship . . . a friend's personal qualities, definition of friendship, overcoming problems with friends

10. Vocabulary development . . . contributions to one's vocabulary, methodology to increase one's vocabulary, courses

4-43. CONSTRUCTING EFFECTIVE TOPIC SENTENCES

These are sample sentences. Students' answers will vary.

1. My father is a conscientious, talented carpenter.
2. Wade Street Middle School offers a challenging and competitive academic program.
3. The camp's sleeping accommodations are antiquated and unsanitary.
4. A trustworthy friend can provide comfort and reliability.
5. Los Angeles is an exciting and interesting entertainment center of the United States.
6. Rome's culture and history attract many tourists.
7. Last Saturday's emotional graduation ceremony provided a time of reflection.
8. Martina's shocking yearbook photographs are a source of concern for our moderator.
9. Newspaper reporting has become more intrusive during the last fifty years.
10. Parents object to the violent shows their children watch.
11. Coach Geiger's demeaning and vitriolic tirades have angered his players.
12. Composition 101 is a demanding course.
13. Our club's leaders are incapable and inefficient.
14. Sitting through that movie was a test of our patience.
15. Marathon running is an extremely challenging physical activity.

4-44. OPENING LINES OF MAGAZINE ARTICLES

Answers may vary, but should be similar to these ideas.

A. 1. the cause of misery
   2. Misery is caused by a mistaken notion.
   3. why we feel we need to be perfect; how we can be happy and still not be perfect
B. 1. When will the next meteor or comet strike the Earth?
   2. There might be another meteor or comet that strikes the Earth.
   3. Why and when another meteor or comet will probably hit the Earth.
C. 1. global trade
   2. Global trade is bringing the people of the world closer.
   3. How global trade is bringing the people closer and closer.

D. 1. white-collar criminals and jail

   2. White-collar criminals should not go to jail.

   3. The reasons why white-collar criminals should not go to jail.

4-45. RECOGNIZING A THESIS STATEMENT

The topic is followed by the opinion.

1. Our last summer vacation . . . difficult time
2. Mr. Kendall's English class . . . test of my patience
3. The 1980s . . . controversial
4. Michael Jordan's retirement . . . time of mixed emotions
5. Jay Leno . . . America's premier comedian
6. My first year at the new school . . . very emotional
7. Lara Thomas . . . biggest influence in my dancing career
8. Senior class members . . . should enjoy off-campus privileges
9. Eating healthy foods . . . major contributor to one's health
10. Capital punishment . . . should be eliminated
11. My mother . . . sweetest woman in the world
12. This activity . . . not that difficult
13. Chicago winters . . . challenge to commuters
14. My Toyota Camry . . . joy to own
15. This room . . . messiest I have ever seen
16. The Quit Smoking program . . . unparalleled success
17. Andrew Lloyd Webber . . . composed some of the world's most beautiful songs
18. This movie . . . not worth the price of admission
19. The *Oxford English Dictionary* . . . great language resource

4-46. IMPROVING THESIS STATEMENTS

The following are sample answers. Students' answers will vary.

1. *Romeo and Juliet* is a story of love and courage.
2. Cheating on school exams is morally and ethically unacceptable.
3. My younger sister is enigmatic.
4. Jake's statement was troublesome and unwarranted.
5. My three cats are both a bane and a blessing.
6. Reagan Brothers Printing is this town's most humane and generous company.
7. Robert Frost's poems "Acquainted with the Night" and "Desert Places" differ in setting and narration.

8. Vinnie's Pizza offers the finest service and the best quality pizza at the most reasonable prices.
9. Miss Melville's social studies class offers little challenge and stimulation.
10. Our two local radio stations play boring, unpopular songs.
11. The neighborhood's violence, location, and residents effected our family's move to this new town.
12. Our government needs to immediately give more assistance to the elderly.
13. Reading is mentally stimulating.
14. *Silent Movie's* premise and dialogue are unique.
15. *M*A*S*H* had clever, humorous dialogue and extremely talented actors.

4-47. FLIPPING THROUGH FOR THE NEXT WRITING

Answers will vary.

4-48. TO THE MARKET WE GO

Dairy items: cheese, eggs, milk, orange juice
Snacks: peanuts, popcorn, potato chips, pretzels
Paper Goods: paper cups, paper napkins, plastic forks, plastic knives
Hygiene items: deodorant, hair spray, nail polish, toothpaste
Meats: chicken, pork chops, roast beef, steak
Fruits: apples, bananas, peaches, pears

4-49. ORGANIZING THE FIVE GROUPS

Astronomy: celestial sphere, eclipse, equinox, quasar, sunspot
Baseball: coach's box, inning, mitt, mound, warning track
Computers: byte, chip, circuit board, monitor, mouse
Housing: apartment, igloo, mansion, split-level, tepee,
Music: chords, concerto, fret, quarter note, rhythm

4-50. SORTING THINGS OUT

Answers will vary.

4-51. MAKING THE CONNECTION

Answers will vary.

4-52. WHAT A YEAR!

These are possible group names and their events (by number).

Sports: 2, 6, 8, 19
Entertainment: 1, 9, 16, 17
Politics: 3, 5, 7, 13, 14, 20
Weather: 11, 15, 18
Business: 4, 10, 12

4-53. WORKING WITH CLUSTERS

Answers will vary.

4-54. MORE WORK WITH CLUSTERS

Answers will vary.

4-55. COMPOSING AN OUTLINE

Answers will vary.

4-56. MAKING SENSE WITH TOPIC OUTLINING

Answers will vary.

4-57. THE MIXED-UP OUTLINE

This is a workable outline. Students could have variations of this outline.
Topic: **A Teacher's Planning for the Academic Year**

  I. Evaluating and Assessing
    A. Self-assessment
    B. Student assessment
      1. Examinations
      2. Observing students
  II. Developing the Year's Curriculum and Activities
    A. Goals and objectives
    B. Selecting and ordering materials

       1. Textbooks

       2. Rubber bands, bulletin board posters

    C. Developing lesson plans—units, weekly, daily

III. Teaching Methods

    A. Lecture

    B. Audio–visual

    C. Discussion

    D. Demonstration

    E. Students teaching other students

IV. Classroom Management

    A. Developing classroom rules and procedures

       1. Homework assignment and collection

       2. Bathroom passes

       3. Lateness

    B. Types of behavior problems

       1. Inappropriate language

       2. Excessive talking

       3. Throwing objects

    C. Punishments for misbehaviors

       1. Detention

       2. Written assignment signed by parent or guardian

       3. Change seat location

       4. Time-out room

4-58. STEPPING INTO ORGANIZATION

Answers will vary.

4-59. PUTTING F. SCOTT FITZGERALD TOGETHER

Answers may vary, but here is one set of possible answers.

Early Years: 1, 5, 7, 8, 9

Personal Life: 2, 11, 12, 14, 15

Writings: 3, 4, 6, 10, 13

4-60. TELL ME A STORY

Answers will vary.

4-61. THE EVENT'S DETAILS

Answers will vary.

4-62. GETTING READY TO WRITE

Answers will vary.

4-63. OBSERVING BEFORE WRITING

Answers will vary.

4-64. CHECKING OUT THE SENTENCES

Here are possible answers.
1. I am (I'm) not going to go there now.
2. He is taller than she.
3. He and I are going to the store very soon.
4. There are several ways to get there.
5. That cat of yours is quite cute.
6. My sister knew that you and I would go with her.
7. Theo likes bowling, skiing, and inline skating.
8. She will stay with them regardless of the repercussions.
9. Will you please get off the ledge?
10. They're (They are) eager to find their way there.
11. Some of the papers are here now.
12. Monica taught me how to drive the automobile.
13. The winners, Ceil and he, are accepting the awards.
14. The record will be broken tomorrow.
15. To whom should I address this package?

4-65. BECOMING MORE SPECIFIC

1. K—EE
2. G—HH
3. E—KK
4. O—DD
5. F—FF
6. I—JJ
7. A—LL
8. D—II
9. M—GG
10. B—BB
11. C—CC
12. L—AA
13. N—OO
14. J—NN
15. H—MM

4-66. MOVING TOWARD PERFECTION

These are possible answers.

General Topic	Specific	More Specific	Most Specific
1. animals	domesticated animals	dogs	collie
2. teachers	academic subjects	science	biology
3. media	television	drama	*ER*
4. furniture	living room furniture	couch	love seat
5. sports	contact sports	football	high school football
6. buildings	brick buildings	library	NYC Public Library
7. entertainment	games	board games	Monopoly®
8. physical activity	running	long-distance running	marathon
9. summer events	picnics	family picnics	Fourth of July picnic
10. workers	indoor workers	secretary	stenographer
11. leaders	political leaders	Canadian political leaders	Brian Mulrooney
12. advertisements	commercials	print ads	IBM ad
13. relatives	male relatives	uncles	Uncle Ed
14. types of writings	personal writings	autobiography	*The Autobiography of Malcolm X*
15. school tests	standardized tests	college admission tests	SAT

4-67. "THE MORE EXACT VERBS" MAGIC SQUARE

A = 13	B = 16	C = 24	D = 2	E = 10
F = 22	G = 5	H = 8	I = 11	J = 19
K = 6	L = 14	M = 17	N = 25	O = 3
P = 20	Q = 23	R = 1	S = 9	T = 12
U = 4	V = 7	W = 15	X = 18	Y = 21

Each row, column, and diagnoal adds up to 65.

4-68. THE DECLARATION OF INDEPENDENCE

Here are acceptable paraphrases. Others may be discussed.

1. God gave all of us certain rights that cannot be taken away.
2. We were taxed against our will.
3. King George III created many new offices and sent his officers here to harass us.
4. King George III has robbed our seas, destroyed our coasts, burned our towns, and destroyed the lives of our people.
5. King George III has captured our citizens on the seas and forced them to fight against their country (America), to kill their friends and brothers/relatives.
6. King George III has not agreed to (okayed) laws that are in the best interest of the people.
7. King George III has instigated internal uprisings here.
8. King George III has made the military independent of and superior to the civil powers (law-abiding agencies).
9. At certain times it is necessary for one group of people to sever the political ties connecting them with another group of people.
10. King George III has called meetings for the legislative bodies in unusual, uncomfortable, and distant locations.

4-69. SAY IT WITHOUT SAYING IT

Answers will vary. These are sample sentences.

1. The proud new mother hugged her giggling baby daughter.
2. Not knowing what to do with the ball, the dribbling guard threw an errant pass.
3. Each child stood open-mouthed as the magician pulled a rabbit from the hat.
4. He refused to become involved in the argument concerning the impeachment.
5. Stirring her coffee in the dimly lit kitchen, the worried mother considered her options.
6. The kindergarten class members frolicked in the leaves during recess.
7. Angry protesters pushed down the embassy's sentinels and rushed into the building.
8. Each day after school, Mrs. Hemingway helped Kent overcome his reading deficiencies.
9. The wealthy woman told the reporter that only "little people" pay taxes.
10. The Welcome Committee members hugged the exchange students at the airport.
11. Jose's parents paced outside the operating room during his brain operation.
12. Seeing his aunt and uncle at the door, five-year-old James jumped up and down.
13. After hearing the umpire's call, the forty-year-old coach sulked on the bench.
14. Holding his burned hand in the air, the welder sought someone's immediate help.
15. Hearing the noise in his darkened basement, Jeremy wished his parents had not gone to the party in the next town.

4-70. DETAILS AND MOOD

Answers will vary.

4-71. ODD ONE OUT

Answers may vary slightly, but should reflect the following.

1. ~~mansion~~; small structures
2. ~~nickel~~; European coins
3. ~~John~~; female names
4. ~~Sugar~~; metals
5. ~~eel~~; snakes
6. ~~egret~~; dogs
7. ~~Mondale~~; U.S. presidents
8. ~~Puppy~~; signs of the Zodiac
9. ~~Toronto~~; Canadian provinces
10. ~~basketball~~; games in which players kick the ball
11. ~~nose~~; things that cover something else
12. ~~"Meet the Press"~~; movies
13. ~~Iceland~~; countries in South America
14. ~~black~~; colors of the spectrum
15. ~~bicycle~~; modes of transportaion propelled by a motor
16. ~~morning~~; seasons
17. ~~cloud~~; places on which a car can travel
18. ~~Mediterranean~~; oceans
19. ~~Fenway Park~~; famous tall buildings
20. ~~blue~~; flavors

4-72. ALL FOUR HAVE IT

These are possible answers. Students may think of others.

Group One: all have four letters; all have two of the same vowel; all have the consonant–vowel–consonant–vowel formation

Group Two: all have six letters; all have the "the" combination; all have an "e"

Group Three: all are state capitals; all begin with the letter "a"; all have a person's name within them (Al, Ann, Gus, Austin)

Group Four: all are played with a round object; all use a net; all have offensive and defensive strategies

Group Five: all float either in water or air; all have four letters; two of the four letters are vowels

Group Six: all are male names; all can add a letter after the last letter to form a new word; all have a vowel surrounded by consonants

Group Seven: all carry one person; all are used to move along on either land or water; all can move quickly

4-73. WHAT DO THEY HAVE IN COMMON?

1. *Alike:* both are used in sports; both can be made of wood

   Different: one is used to hit a ball, the other to catch a ball; one does not have netting

2. *Alike:* both (usually) have five digits; both have one digit that does not look much like the other four digits

   Different: one is used primarily for grasping, the other primarily for walking; one has much more flexibility

3. *Alike:* both are used for recording; both can skip from overuse

   Different: you can't usually see a CD when it is playing, but you generally see the vinyl record; you do not have to replace a needle with a CD

4. *Alike:* both have four legs; both have hair

   Different: one can be kept indoors (excluding barns); one can be ridden

5. *Alike:* both have been very good in their respective sports; both are very popular

   Different: one is male and one is female; one is American and one is Russian

6.–10. Answers will vary.

4-74. WRITING HEADLINES AND SUMMARIES

Answers will vary.

4-75. HOW TO PRESENT IT

Answers will vary.

4-76. START WITH THIS

Answers will vary.

4-77. HERE IS YOUR LIFE

Answers will vary.

4-78. TODAY'S JOURNAL

Answers will vary.

4-79. FREE WRITING

Answers will vary.

4-80. JOURNAL WRITING

Answers will vary, but they should reflect events/topics included in the sample journal entry.

4-81. BEING THERE

Answers will vary.

4-82. ORGANIZING SOME WRITING SITUATIONS

Answers will vary. Here are some possible subtopics.

1. age, physical features, intellectual abilities, personality traits
2. age, physical features, location, grade levels of students in the school
3. title of movie, cast members, production costs, plot, type (mystery, romance, etc.)
4. cost, location, sleeping arrangements, travel arrangements
5. cost of purchase, maintenance costs, appearance, accessories
6. land, air, water, land and water, automatic, motorized
7. jazz, rock, country, instrumental, reggae, rap, blues
8. white-collar, blue-collar, manual, professional
9. written, visual, audio, audio–visual
10. oceans, seas, rivers, lakes, streams

4-83. KNOWING YOUR AUDIENCE

Answers will vary.

4-84. HERE'S A START

Answers will vary.

4-85. WHICH WRITING METHOD?

Answers will vary.

4-86. IDEAS FOR COMPARING AND CONTRASTING

Answers will vary.

4-87. SENSORY DESCRIPTIONS

Answers will vary.

4-88. PLEASE EXPLAIN HOW TO DO IT

Answers will vary.

4-89. THE PERSUASIVE ESSAY

Answers will vary.

4-90. WHAT IF?

Answers will vary.